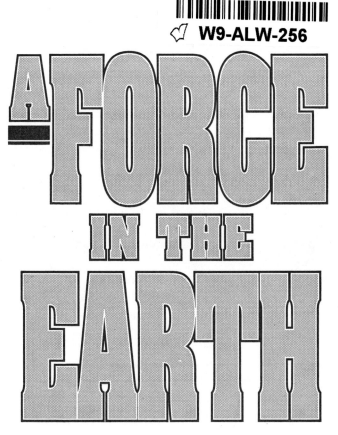

A FORCE IN THE EARTH

The Charismatic Renewal and World Evangelism

DAVID SHIBLEY

Foreword by C. PETER WAGNER

Creation House
Altamonte Springs, Florida

Creation House
Strang Communications Company
600 Rinehart Road
Lake Mary, FL 32746

Unless otherwise noted, all Scripture quotations are taken
from the New King James Version. Copyright © 1979, 1980,
1982, Thomas Nelson Inc., Publishers. Used by permission.
Scripture quotations marked NIV are taken from the Holy
Bible, New International Version. Copyright © 1973, 1978,
1984, International Bible Society. Used by permission.

Missionaries must be absolutely united
in the conviction that world evangelization is a
divine enterprise, that the Spirit of God is the great
missioner, and that only as He dominates
the work and workers can we hope for success in
the undertaking to carry the knowledge
of Christ to all people.
—*John R. Mott*

Contents

Foreword

The book you are about to read is a powerhouse. It will certainly take its place as one of the missions publication events of these days. *A Force in the Earth* is a bright spotlight that illumines one of the most significant historical hinges in the Christian movement.

The great new fact of Christianity since World War II is the unprecedented burgeoning of the Pentecostal and charismatic movements. David Barrett ranks it as an ecclesiastical mega-trend. I do not believe I exaggerate when I say that throughout human history no other nonpolitical, nonmilitaristic, voluntary movement has grown as fast as the Pentecostal/charismatic movement over the past quarter-century.

David Shibley writes out of a charismatic milieu. While classical Pentecostals have effectively mobilized for world missions, charismatics, representing a newer wave of the Holy Spirit, have up to now been struggling with their role as a "force in the earth." The question has not involved the charismatics' *desire* to be a force for world evangelization; it has revolved around their *ability* to mobilize, structure and act effectively. How can this great, young, vigorous, spiritual force be all that God wants it to be in fulfilling Jesus' Great Commission?

David Shibley points the way. This is the book that pastors, mission leaders and lay people who want to give their all for God have been waiting for. *A Force in the Earth* will move you profoundly because it is:

Biblical. The book emerges from sound theological roots. You will feel God's heart for finding the lost in the Old Testament as well as the New Testament.

Informed. Thorough research underlies this book. Through these pages you will meet many of the great contemporary mission leaders and absorb their vision for the gospel moving to the ends of the earth.

Optimistic. David Shibley believes that the task can be completed by A.D. 2000. He says, "What a great day to be a Christian!" Before you finish this book, you will be saying, "Amen!"

Ecumenical. The author is a charismatic, but he refuses to put himself in a box. He loves the whole body of Christ and sees himself moving with, not against, brothers and sisters from other traditions.

Humble. Readers who represent other traditions will find that David Shibley does not say that to win the world you should be like us or do it our way. Instead he says that noncharismatics will not do it well without charismatics; neither will charismatics do it well without noncharismatics.

I am planning to use this as a textbook in my classes

at Fuller Seminary. I will tell my students that they must read it because it is a book of *passion*—passion for saving the lost; it is a book of *prayer*—showing how the Lord's prayer is a missionary challenge; and it is a book of *power*—the power of the Holy Spirit moving through His people so that they can be "a force in the earth."

And that is also why I recommend it to you.

C. Peter Wagner
Fuller Seminary School of World Mission
Pasadena, California

ONE

Why World Missions?

*There is no argument for missions. The total
action of God in history, the whole revelation
of God in Christ—this is the argument.*
                                    —James S. Stewart

Blame this on my father," I blurted as I hung my
head on the steering wheel of our car and sobbed.
Naomi and I had just made a quick exit from
the little apartment of furloughed missionary friends.
Throughout the evening as they had graciously served
dinner to my wife and me, I had fought to keep my emotions in check. Weakened by a lack of funds and tropical
diseases, they had recently returned from Liberia. They
were in the States "for as little time as possible," the
man told us. "As soon as we can, we want to go

11

back home to Africa.''

Though I tried not to show it, their love for Jesus and the world He died to save overwhelmed me. Finally, in the privacy of our car, I broke down. Half-joking I explained the outburst to Naomi: "I guess this is my dad's fault." With a tear-stained smile I recalled my missions heritage.

My father, Warren Shibley, is now home in heaven. He was affectionately known to many as "the man with a missionary heart." From day one, the church he pastored gave 50 percent of its income to missions. It was not unusual for me to awaken late at night and hear him praying for nations, missionaries and needed finances for missions projects. Somehow his love for world missions was injected in me.

Neither my mother nor I was expected to survive my birth. As my mother was in labor, my father waited anxiously with a family friend, T.L. Osborn, a noted evangelist used as few others in overseas crusades. Osborn was strongly impressed to pray for my life and my mother's. Turning to my father, he said, "Warren, we've got to rebuke the spirit of death right now."

God intervened. What appeared to be certain death for both mother and child (who weighed under four pounds) was turned into victory and honor for the Lord. Today I enjoy consistently good health. And my mother, now seventy, does the work of any two other persons as my secretary. On a human level, we may owe our lives to the sensitivity and faith of a missionary-evangelist.

Long before my mother was my secretary, she was T.L. Osborn's secretary. At first the records of his young ministry were kept in our spare bedroom. But when I came home from the hospital, that room became my nursery. Osborn soon acquired his first office on North Utica Street in Tulsa.

My parents, members of the board of the Osborn ministries, sometimes took me as a child to the board meetings. While I played in the corner, my subconscious mind absorbed the hum of their optimistic discussions about world evangelism. I remember T.L. Osborn coming back from his now historic crusades with a passion for souls in his eyes. We wept as we watched the pagan rituals captured on raw footage that would later become his classic missionary films.

You see, world missions was woven into the fabric of my Pentecostal upbringing. So some of the teaching of the seventies and eighties, suggesting that we should heap blessings on ourselves instead of a needy world, sounded shrill to my ears. In my family's framework of faith, all we had was for the benefit of others who didn't have. With the apostle Paul, we sensed an acute debt to bring the gospel and its attendant blessings to our generation. In fact, my mother tells me that the first song I went around the house singing was "Send the Light"!

We knew God had put us here for a purpose. We were people of destiny. God had raised up simple, full-gospel folks like us to be a force in the earth.

For Such a Time as This

Something historic is happening. All across the world Christians are sensing that this is God's hour for global harvest. Every major stream of Christendom is pointing toward the year 2000 as a target for fulfilling Christ's Great Commission. The converging of events and people toward completing the task is unprecedented.

The twentieth century began with an outpouring of the Holy Spirit. From Topeka, Kansas, and a little mission on Azusa Street in Los Angeles, reports of recurrences of New Testament gifts began to filter out. Parallel with this fresh outbreak of spiritual dynamism, there was a renewed call for "the evangelization of the world in this generation."

Now, as we race toward a new century and millennium, we see a new surge of God's power. This time, however, the phenomenon is not limited to a Bible school in a wheat field and a storefront mission. The reverberations of God's power are worldwide. And the missions battle cry has become more distinct: world evangelization not in this generation but in this *decade*.

We are closer than ever to the realization of God's ancient promise to Joel: "I will pour out My Spirit on all flesh" (Joel 2:28). For the first time in history, the total evangelization of this planet is more than a pipe dream. True, the population is larger than ever. The opposition is stronger than ever. Yet the resources to finish the job are greater than ever.

What part has God ordained for Spirit-renewed Christians to play in the global harvest? Why have we been entrusted with heaven's power? What about the large charismatic churches that have sprouted in the eighties? Were they birthed simply to bless their own constituents? Or does God have some bigger, more noble design?

Mordecai reminded his niece, Queen Esther, that she had been brought to the kingdom "for such a time as this" (Esth. 4:14). God had sovereignly intersected Esther's life with a one-chance, go-for-broke, win-it-all-or-lose-it-all situation. Just so, God has sovereignly orchestrated events to mesh a worldwide renewal with a once-in-a-millennium opportunity. By sovereign grace, it has fallen on our generation to have within our grasp that for which other generations of Christians could only dream—closure on world evangelization.

We in the charismatic renewal must always be careful to remember the immense debt we owe to our traditional evangelical brothers and sisters. Traditional evangelicals have most often been in the forefront of world missions since the world-Christian movement began to regather steam some two hundred years ago. Yet, while we always acknowledge with gratitude to God the pioneering work of the other evangelicals, we must humbly yet honestly ask who is best suited to invade the final frontiers. Surely it will take supernatural spiritual dynamics to break through the obstacles preventing the final ingathering. Not long ago a young man approached Vinson Synan, a respected leader in the Holy Spirit renewal, with a word he felt was from the Lord regarding the role charismatics are to play in world evangelization. The message is profound in its simplicity: "If not us, who? If not now, when?"

From its humble beginnings at the turn of the century, the movement of the Holy Spirit has grown to become the most vital force in Christianity today. By 1988 there were some 332 million Spirit-renewed Christians in 230 countries. Today 21 percent of all Christian church members worldwide are part of this renewal. According to missiologist David Barrett's figures for 1988, there are five million "Prepentecostals" identified with various holiness groups. Pentecostals, both classical and independent, number 176 million. Another 123 million could be termed charismatic. These charismatic Christians are found in all Protestant denominations, the Orthodox and Catholic churches and independent, nonaligned fellowships. The relatively new phenomenon of the "third wave" (evangelicals who shun charismatic or Pentecostal labels but embrace all gifts of the Spirit as vital for ministry today) has emerged with another 28 million adherents.[1]

Barrett categorizes these different streams of the Holy Spirit's renewal with terminology popularized by Peter Wagner. Wagner describes the initial outbreak of the Pentecostal revival at the beginning of this century as the "first wave." The charismatic movement, which emerged in the sixties among both Protestants and Catholics, comprises the "second wave." The third wave is made up of evangelicals, many of whom were resistant to the first and second waves theologically or culturally. Now they believe all gifts of the Spirit mentioned in Scripture are operative today. In fact, they welcome getting in on the action themselves (minus the cultural baggage of the previous movements).

What one terms himself or herself or wishes to be termed is not important. What *is* important is that one is flowing in the present-day power of the Holy Spirit. God's Spirit is ever pointing in one direction—toward

the preeminence of Jesus Christ. And He is ever pressing us toward one great goal—the fulfillment of the Great
Commission. For the first time since the first century,
the evangelization of the world is within our grasp. We
have been brought to the kingdom for such a time as this.

God's Eternal Purpose

God's interest in redeeming humanity did not begin
when Jesus issued the Great Commission to His followers. Yet some seem to feel that Jesus added this
command almost as an addendum—a P.S. before His
ascension. Some apparently believe He was just about
airborne when He screeched to a halt and said, "Oh,
by the way, go into all the world and preach the gospel."

Far from it! Jesus left the Great Commission as His
last words on earth to underscore, not diminish, its
importance. He was echoing the heartbeat of His Father:
an aggressive compassion that had always characterized
God's dealing with humanity.

After their sin Adam and Eve experienced the natural
consequence of their rebellion: a desire to hide from
God. But the Father-heart of God came calling. God
employed an aggressive "evangelistic" strategy as He
lovingly forced our first parents to face their sin. From
the moment mankind's fellowship with the Creator was
broken, God has been in the business of restoring it.

For the expressed purpose of showering His mercy
on all families of earth, God called out a man named
Abram. God covenanted to bless him, again for a
specific purpose. "Get out of your country," God told
him, "from your kindred and from your father's house,

to a land that I will show you. I will make you a great nation; I will bless you and make your name great; and you shall be a blessing....And in you all the families of the earth shall be blessed'' (Gen. 12:1-3).

Notice that God promised to bless Abram in the context of radical obedience, as He called Abram to be the world's first cross-cultural missionary. It is in the arena of sacrificial risk that God's blessing comes.

Some of us might be prone to receive the promise of blessing and leave it at that. ''I will bless you and make your name great.'' Period. That's the promise we would stick on our refrigerators. But look at *why* God promised to bless Abram: ''I will bless you and make your name great; *and you shall be a blessing.*'' God blesses us so we may bless others.

Do you consider the knowledge of Jesus a blessing? I'm sure you do. Why, then, has this blessing been given to you? We have been blessed with the gospel that we might bless others with the gospel. We have been blessed so we might be a blessing. We've heard plenty in the last few years about our ''right'' to be blessed. But we have heard precious little about our responsibility to be a blessing. Let's never forget that God's blessings are never to stop with us; they are to reverberate through us to all the families of the earth.

From Abram (later named Abraham) a seed came that would bring universal blessing. The Bible is clear that the seed of blessing is Jesus Christ. But Christ came in human flesh through a specific ''line of faith'' from Abraham. This line of faith, from which the Messiah would one day appear, began with Abraham's son Isaac.

From Isaac a nation was born. This nation was to bear God's light and truth to all surrounding peoples. A very clear commission was given to ancient Israel: "Declare His glory among the nations, His wonders among all peoples" (Ps. 96:3). Far from being a tribal deity of the Hebrews, God pronounced His intention to be worshipped for who He is: King of the universe. The ancient nation of Israel was to be His agent to bring all nations to worship Him.

Somewhere along the line, however, the people of God distorted the commission. Instead of seeing their neighbors as potential converts for the one true God, they viewed them with suspicion and even hatred. Instead of being a light to surrounding nations, Israel was riddled with provincialism, ethnic pride and a protectionist mentality.

By the time of Christ, the people once called to be God's light to the nations had retreated into enclaves of religious arrogance.

The Bible's Integrating Theme

A new covenant between God and His people was established through Christ. Under the new covenant, the children of God are those who receive His Son and believe on His name for salvation. The commission once given to Israel to be God's light to the nations has now been transferred to His new-covenant people, the church.

The Great Commission appears in some form in each of the Gospels and in the book of Acts. In Matthew 28:18-20 Jesus commands His disciples to disciple all nations. In Mark 16:15-18 Jesus tells us to go into all the world, preaching His good news to everyone. He promises that wonderful signs will attend the preaching of the gospel. In Luke 24:46-48 Jesus says that repentance and remission of sins are to be preached in His name to all nations. In John 20:21 the Savior extends His own commission to His followers: "As the Father has sent Me, I also send you."

This Great Commission, given by Christ to those who follow Him, is not just a nice suggestion. It is an order issued by our resurrected Lord. But how can we do it? What resource is there for such a colossal assignment? Again Jesus points the way. In Acts 1:8 He promises, "But you shall receive power when the Holy Spirit has come upon you; and you shall be witnesses to Me in Jerusalem, and in all Judea and Samaria, and to the end of the earth." When we talk of world evangelization we are talking about a supernatural enterprise that can only be accomplished by the enduement of supernatural power.

The Bible's integrating theme is the awesome story of how God Himself intervened to save His fallen creation, bent on self-destruction. W.A. Criswell, long-time pastor of the First Baptist Church in Dallas, says, "The scarlet thread of redemption runs through the Bible." God's eternal purpose is to call out a bride for His Son from fallen humanity. The composition of this bride will be redeemed humanity "out of *every* tribe and tongue and people and nation" (Rev. 5:9). As my beloved friend Paul Billheimer observed, "There is romance at the heart of the universe."

The Father-heart of God bleeds through all of

Scripture. The missionary mandate is not confined to the Great Commission passages. Paul, who said we were to "owe no one anything" (Rom. 13:8), said in the same book that he had incurred an acute debt.

> I am a debtor both to Greeks and to barbarians, both to wise and to unwise.
>
> So, as much as is in me, I am ready to preach the gospel to you who are in Rome also.
>
> For I am not ashamed of the gospel of Christ, for it is the power of God to salvation for everyone who believes, for the Jew first and also for the Greek (Rom. 1:14-16).

Paul had a keen, innate awareness that he owed his generation the good news.

Peter as well understood that God's great longing is to redeem humankind. In fact, the whole timetable for Christ's return is somehow tied to ensuring that the last person in the global family of faith is brought in. "The Lord is not slack concerning His promise, as some count slackness, but is longsuffering toward us, not willing that any should perish but that all should come to repentance" (2 Pet. 3:9).

The writer of Hebrews says that, because of Christ's sacrifice, the potential of redemption reaches every person on the planet. "But we see Jesus, who was made a little lower than the angels, for the suffering of death crowned with glory and honor, that He, by the grace of God, might taste death for everyone" (Heb. 2:9).

The Bible is so abundantly laced with the missions mandate that Ralph Winter, founder of the U.S. Center for World Mission, objects to the term "the biblical basis of missions." Winter contends that the Bible itself is the basis of missions!

Because of man's rebellion against God, Satan wreaked havoc over humanity. Romans 6:23 says, "The wages of sin is death," physically, spiritually and culturally. In His immense mercy, God has intervened through Jesus Christ and stripped Satan of all authority. By legal right, Jesus Christ is now ruler over this planet. "The earth is the Lord's, and all its fullness, the world and those who dwell therein" (Ps. 24:1). Redemption means to purchase again. Jesus has purchased us. He has redeemed us from Satan's grip. Now He has let us get in on the greatest privilege on earth. We are urged to go on a rescue mission with Him, bringing the good news of liberty from Satan's bondage to a humanity still in chains.

Why Now?

We've just seen a very brief, biblical rationale for involvement in God's master purpose. His master purpose is to bring all of planet Earth under the full reign of Jesus Christ. That is where history is moving. As Christians obedient to Christ's command, we are assisting in moving history in that direction.

The challenge of missions is nothing new. But why is the Holy Spirit spotlighting missions now? As I travel across America and around the world, I've been heartened to see a potent groundswell of missions interest in the last few years. Why, suddenly and dramatically, are we turning from the self-serving teachings of the eighties to a message with global implications?

First, and perhaps foremost, we are living in a season the Bible would describe as the fullness of time. Throughout history God has made major transitions in His dealings with humanity in two-thousand-year increments. This leads many Christians to believe that extremely momentous events are about to occur. As we approach the year 2000, we need to remember that this will not be merely the turning of a decade. It will not even be just the turning of a century. It will be the turning of a millennium! This has occurred only one other time in history since the advent of Christ.

For roughly two thousand years the church has been under mandate to disciple all nations. Yet we have not reached the known world with the gospel. But *now*, for the first time in two millennia, almost every major stream of Christianity is giving world evangelization top priority. The evangelical wing of the church is redoubling its missions efforts. Classical Pentecostals refer to the nineties as the decade of harvest. Evangelical charismatics are uniting with their brothers and sisters in unity for the global task. Renewal-oriented Christians, both Protestant and Catholic, have joined in a massive effort called AD 2000 Together.

Many mission agencies are targeting for world evangelization by that date. Every Home for Christ (formerly World Literature Crusade) is well on its way to its goal of establishing a functioning base of systematic literature evangelism in every nation by the year 2000. I serve on their board of directors, and already 1.6 billion gospel messages have been distributed systematically, house to house, in 101 nations. Campus Crusade for Christ is sponsoring New Life 2000, aiming to show their *Jesus* film worldwide and to plant churches among converts. Major missionary radio networks are cooperating to blanket the earth with the gospel through a joint effort dubbed World by 2000. Southern Baptists are committed to Bold Mission Thrust, a plan to reach everyone with the gospel in the next decade. And charismatic Roman Catholics have earmarked $100 million for Evangelization 2000, an aggressive plan to give Jesus a present of a world at least 50 percent Christian on His two thousandth birthday.

What a great day to be a Christian! Just think of it. Dwight L. Moody is gone. Charles Spurgeon is gone. David Livingstone is gone. But *you* have been allowed to live now to see potential fulfillment of the Great Commission. The Bible says that many good people, even prophets, desired to see the things we now see. For sovereign reasons known only to Him, your life is intersecting with unprecedented events.

There will never be a better time to finish the job. Without sounding melodramatic, I could argue that, if we fail, the church could plunge into a second "dark ages." When we look at the immensity of the task, our hearts cry, "Lord, who is sufficient for these things?" Yet we remember that nothing—including the evangelization of the world—is too hard for God. "But we have this treasure in earthen vessels, that the excellence of the power may be of God and not of us" (2 Cor. 4:7). If not us, who? If not now, when?

TWO

Missions' Awakening Giant

In essentials, unity; in nonessentials, liberty; in all things, charity.　　　　　*—Augustine*

A few years ago I had dinner with Dick Mills. Since I respected Dick as an incisive thinker and anointed minister, I wanted to probe his mind and heart.

"Tell me, Dick," I inquired, "what is the Holy Spirit saying to the charismatic movement today regarding missions?"

"Not much," he replied, "because they're not listening."

I was startled by his answer. Yet I knew it was often

true. For years charismatics—especially independents—were the sleeping giant of world missions. But, thank God, that giant is waking up. Today, as always, the Holy Spirit is speaking to us about our global responsibility. And now, more than ever, we are listening. By the way, I saw Dick Mills recently, and he rejoices with me in this dramatic change of heart.

The Charismatic Factor

There is a great new fact of missions that must be confronted. The whole church must acknowledge it, whether it represents their wishes or not. Some charismatics will not appreciate the first assertion; some old-line evangelicals will not warm to the second. Nevertheless, the fact remains: *World evangelization can never be accomplished by charismatics alone. Neither can it be realized without us.*

It is insensitive and plainly illogical for charismatics to think they do not need the rest of the body of Christ in fulfilling the Great Commission. Recently a friend asked me, "Why wouldn't it be possible for charismatics to do it alone?"

My answer was, "The Holy Spirit wouldn't allow it." The first half of the eighties brought explosive growth to independent charismatic churches. The last half of the eighties saw us chastened for our arrogance. Among the many lessons God is teaching us, we are learning that we are not a law unto ourselves. We are learning our interdependence on the rest of the body of Christ.

At the same time, traditional evangelicals are now realizing they cannot hide behind their missiological expertise and pretend they do not need the charismatic element. Let's be honest. Charismatics need the academic and theological strength the evangelicals provide. And traditional evangelicals need the fire and faith charismatics bring. The Bible says, "We are members of one another" (Eph. 4:25).

Unity is a sticky question. Every Christian struggles to relate correctly to the rest of the church. On the one hand, it is important for us to sense personal ownership of the Great Commission. We must feel an urgency that stretches us to work as if no one else were working to spread the gospel. Yet we must be humble enough and realistic enough to understand that world evangelization is a cooperative effort.

I am convinced of this: If fulfilling Christ's Great Commission were possible without the cooperation of the charismatic wing of the church, it would have happened already. Certainly there is no lack of sincerity among traditional evangelicals for world evangelization. Many of these evangelical mission agencies are decades ahead of most charismatics in missions expertise and sacrificial life-styles. What is missing, then, must be some other ingredient.

Although I identify with the charismatic wing of the church, I also consider myself an evangelical. I am a charismatic evangelical; the adjective further describes the noun. As a born-again Christian I espouse everything theologically that most evangelicals endorse. Experientially, however, I am a charismatic. I believe the gifts of the Holy Spirit are vital for the success of evangelism in our day.

Still I would never discount the importance of proclamation evangelism. To preach the gospel, under the Spirit's anointing, is the essence of evangelism. The *kerugma*, the saving activity of God in Christ, is precious to all Christians. Proclamation evangelism is represented by Billy Graham, Luis Palau and others. Their sterling character is a powerful component of their ministries. The long-term integrity of these and other evangelicals is very attractive to many non-Christians.

In the last decade charismatics gave heavy emphasis to faith. This was good. Without question it will take gargantuan faith to open the massive blocks of humanity that now seem closed to the gospel. Sadly, however, we often released our faith in wrong directions—not toward the nations but toward building personal empires.

This underscores the importance of what we stress theologically. During the eighties, we stressed faith and that is exactly what we got. We produced people of astounding vision who dared to tackle anything. But our emphasis on faith was sometimes at the expense of an emphasis on godly character. Consequently, we produced visionary heavyweights and character bantamweights. The very empires that were built by faith became crushing burdens, because they did not have sufficient character to undergird them. Clearly some charismatics have needed lessons in character from their traditional evangelical counterparts.

Having said this, it remains true that proclamation alone will not get the job done in many parts of the world. Most of the human family has a supernatural orientation. If we bring them a Christianity devoid of verifying power, many will perceive our message only as one of many competing, moralistic philosophies.

This is where charismatics can and must make a major contribution to world evangelization. We are needed, first and foremost, because only the power of the Holy Spirit, complete with signs and wonders, can penetrate the final frontiers. The strongholds of ancient religions can be torn down only through spiritual warfare. The militance of Islam can be countered only by supernatural phenomena. Tribal addiction to demon spirits can be broken only by the power of the Holy Spirit.

Charismatics are also vital to world evangelization because of their sheer numbers. In 1975 there were 61 million Pentecostals and charismatics worldwide. Ten years later that number had nearly tripled to 169 million. Some say it may be closer to 200 million, if we knew how to count China correctly. The fastest growing church segment in America today is the independent charismatic churches, with more than eighty thousand congregations, most of which have started since 1980.

Clearly, such a colossal force cannot be ignored. But we charismatics need to remember that we are not the entire picture. Not by a long shot. So let me say it again: World evangelization can never be accomplished by charismatics alone. Neither can it be realized without us.

"That the World May Believe"

In Jesus' great prayer for His followers, He prayed that they would experience oneness of heart. He prayed "that they all may be one, as You, Father, are in Me, and I in You; that they also may be one in Us, that the world may believe that You sent Me'' (John 17:21). Notice that our Lord's prayer for unity was for a distinct purpose: that the world may believe in Him. Unity is not an end in itself. The true goal of Christian unity is world evangelization.

We must walk cautiously here. What kind of unity are we speaking of? And what kind of dynamic brings it about? Here we need to take some lessons from history.

Many people today do not realize that the foundations for the World Council of Churches were drenched in missionary passion. The hearts of great men such as John R. Mott longed for a more visible expression of Christian unity than existed at that time among many denominations. As these men traveled, they saw the embarrassment caused by a fractured Christianity. They perceived disunity as the chief impediment to world evangelization. The Edinburgh World Missionary Conference, convened in 1910, was a landmark because it was the first truly interdenominational missions conference. The networking that began there helped spawn the World Council of Churches several years later.

Sadly, many in the WCC have lost sight of its missions base. Salvation itself is now often defined not as a personal spiritual transformation but as the redemption of society through political and educational reforms. Unity has degenerated into a goal in itself. Some have so marred the biblical mandate as to say that Christian unity will mirror the unity of humankind, no matter what a person's religion.

Evangelicals, both charismatic and noncharismatic,

denounce complicity based on compromise of the gospel. There is only one road to God. We affirm, with Peter, "Nor is there salvation in any other, for there is no other name under heaven given among men by which we must be saved" (Acts 4:12). We ascribe to the words of Jesus Himself: "I am the way, the truth, and the life. No one comes to the Father except through Me" (John 14:6). God has no Plan B for salvation. Jesus Christ is the way.

This is not to say that our posture is retreat from others, as some fundamentalists have chosen. Rather it means that we understand what unity is—and what it is not.

I believe the unity of believers for which Jesus prayed is spiritual, not organizational. God Himself is infinitely diverse in His creation; it is His one creation but it is expressed in many beautifully different ways. In the same way, Christ's church is one. We share in common "one body and one Spirit...one hope...one Lord, one faith, one baptism; one God and Father of all" (Eph. 4:4-6). It is a unity we share in the Spirit, and it doesn't come naturally. It comes supernaturally. We are to be "endeavoring to keep the unity of the Spirit in the bond of peace" (Eph. 4:3). It is something toward which we must constantly work.

The unity of Christians under the new covenant should parallel the unity of the children of Israel under the old covenant. In the everyday functions of life, they were twelve distinct tribes. They guarded distinct tribal customs. They usually married within the tribe. Their sense of community was first related to their tribe. At times, however, this mind-set was radically changed. If any tribe of Israel experienced aggression from the outside, the other tribes immediately came to its defense. They no longer viewed themselves as separate tribes; they were one nation of Israel.

In the same way, we are free as Christians to pursue community in that group into which we are led by the Spirit and in which we feel most "at home." However, when any part of the body of Christ is assaulted, our labels cease to be important. We share as one the common future of Christians worldwide. For many, our denominational tags are becoming less important. Other Christians are increasingly unaffected even by the designations of "charismatic" or "Pentecostal" or "evangelical." We simply wish to be world Christians. Our first line of identification is with the body of Christ worldwide, especially those in every nation who share our passion for closure on the Great Commission.

I realize this is unnerving to some of my charismatic brothers and sisters. For years there has been a kind of charismatic *koinonia*, a fellowship based on the baptism in the Holy Spirit. Now, however, I find my closest heart identification with "world Christians," Christians whose heartbeat is world evangelization, whether they are charismatics or traditional evangelicals, regardless of their nationality.

Biblical unity is not a person-enforced conformity but a Spirit-orchestrated cooperation. Unity at any price is no more desirable than peace at any price. At the same time, unity for the purpose of gospel advancement is worth the deference it will take to achieve it. The slogan of the Association of International Mission Services says it well: "Unity in the Spirit for world evangelization."

Since its inception almost thirty years ago, the charismatic movement has been a catalyst for Christian unity. Whereas the starting point of evangelical unity is common adherence to a doctrinal position, charismatic unity begins with being born again and is followed by a common experience of baptism in the Holy Spirit. This has allowed us to have a vast base of cooperation since the fire of the Spirit has leaped across denominational and sectarian boundaries. Evangelical well-wishers have pointed out that this also may be our greatest weakness. Fellowship based on the least common denominator is not necessarily strong. It is true that our inclusive tendencies have sometimes produced theological flabbiness.

The one common confession around which charismatics have convened in conferences, churches and evangelistic efforts is "Jesus is Lord." True, this statement settles no debates regarding modes of baptism, eschatology or church polity. It does, however, provide a central reference in a Person and in His supremacy. We acknowledge the cautions of our evangelical brethren. We admit that our lack of theological acumen has sometimes brought acute embarrassment. Nevertheless, I'm sure they would agree that a simple, experiential confession of the lordship of Christ is preferable to dead orthodoxy.

The charismatic movement has a lot of warts. Still, it is an amazing spiritual phenomenon. Never in history has there been such a broad base for evangelistic cooperation. It would not have been possible to pull so many streams together in a traditional evangelical framework. But because of a unity in the Spirit, charismatic Catholics, mainline Protestant charismatics, third-wave evangelicals, independent charismatics and traditional Pentecostals all sense some level of an over-arching, "mystic, sweet communion."

Charismatic unity is different by definition from the union of church communions found in liberal circles. Charismatic unity is "unity in the Spirit." Over the almost three decades of this movement, I have never heard anyone propose a "charismatic movement denomination." Rather Spirit-renewed believers have been urged to go back into existing church structures as agents of life. Even those who have founded independent charismatic groups do not see them as encompassing the entire movement.

I believe God was behind this Spirit-induced co-operation. His purpose was to provide a spiritual framework for the accomplishment of His purpose in this generation. For many years charismatics spoke only of "unity in the Spirit." Now, thank God, a new element is being added. God is bringing unity in the Spirit *for world evangelization*. The theme of the massive charismatic conference in New Orleans in 1987 was "The Holy Spirit and World Evangelization." This signalled a new era. It was the first time charismatics had said in the theme of a major convention what all this power is for.

If the charismatic movement provides a spiritual framework for cooperation toward world evangelization, the Lausanne Covenant provides the theological framework. Drafted at the 1974 International Congress on World Evangelization at Lausanne, Switzerland, it has become a rallying point for all kinds of evangelicals. John R.W. Stott was the covenant's chief architect. It is a masterful blend of clear evangelical theology in an ecumenical spirit. Its purpose appears to be to express the sentiments of as large a segment of the body of Christ as possible regarding evangelism without surrendering basic biblical truths.

The covenant speaks directly to the issue of cooperation in evangelism in an eloquent paragraph:

> We affirm that the church's visible unity in truth is God's purpose. Evangelism also summons us to unity, because our oneness strengthens our witness, just as our disunity undermines our Gospel of reconciliation. We recognize, however, that organizational unity may take many forms and does not necessarily forward evangelism. Yet we who share the same biblical faith should be closely united in fellowship, work and witness. We confess that our testimony has sometimes been marred by sinful individualism and needless duplication. We pledge ourselves to seek a deeper unity in truth, worship, holiness and mission. We urge the development of regional and functional cooperation for the furtherance of the church's mission, for strategic planning, for mutual encouragement, and for the sharing of resources and experience.

The Changing Complexion of the Global Church

I wrote *A Charismatic Truce* in 1978 because I was

distressed by the rampant disunity I saw. Both charismatics and traditional evangelicals had mastered the fine art of creating straw men of one another. Then they proceeded to destroy the caricature they had created. The book was a plea for tolerance between traditional evangelicals and charismatics to bring about a more united witness for Christ.

Much has happened since then. While some evangelicals may still wish they could, it is increasingly difficult to avoid the pervasive presence of charismatic Christians. In college I read an editorial in a well-known Christian periodical. The article stated that, by the start of the next century, the church essentially would be comprised of a modified charismatic Protestantism and a modified charismatic Catholicism. At the time, in 1972, I considered the prediction almost absurd. Today I consider it quite possibly prophetic.

The first Lausanne International Congress on World Evangelization hardly mentioned Pentecostals or charismatics. The 1989 Lausanne congress in Manila featured an entire track of workshops dealing with the relation of signs and wonders to evangelism, casting out demons, coming against principalities and powers in intercession, and the role of the Holy Spirit in missions. A staff member of the Lausanne committee told me that nearly 50 percent of the participants had some kind of charismatic orientation.

David Barrett estimates that roughly 80 percent of all conversions in frontier areas are the result of some full-gospel missionary effort. Evidently, there has been a dramatic shift in the past several years. Whereas evangelicals have spearheaded most great missions endeavors for the last two hundred years, this may be shifting to the charismatic wing of the church.

If this is true, it should not be a cause for pride among charismatics. If we are seeing further than our predecessors (which is debatable), it is because we are standing on the shoulders of evangelical giants who gave their entire lives to advance the gospel. Generally, charismatics are not the statisticians, academicians and missiologists. We are the visionaries and plodders. We need one another. This generation is better equipped for missions academically than any previous generation. But we are often more poorly equipped emotionally. We must recapture the passion of former days to reach the last, the least, the lost. This is where charismatics can make a strong contribution. We are missions' awakening giant.

As the Lausanne Covenant states, "...the whole church must take the whole Gospel to the whole world." In this greatest and most noble of tasks, we are laborers together with God. *World evangelization can never be accomplished by charismatics alone. Neither can it be accomplished without us.*

THREE

The Role of Power Evangelism

It is "this gospel of the kingdom," preached in the power of God, confirmed by signs and wonders and divers miracles, that always produces the greatest evangelistic triumphs in any generation.
                                              —T.L. Osborn

The young man raced toward the crusade platform, hands raised to heaven, tears and a broad smile gracing his face. It was the second night of an evangelistic crusade I was conducting in Nigeria. "I've lived with constant pain in my back for the last five years," he shouted to the crowd. "I'm born and raised a Muslim but *this Jesus* has healed me. The pain is gone. I must become a Christian!"

Shouts of joy echoed through the crowd. We had experienced a supernatural breakthrough. As a result, several hundred people responded to Christ.

If Barrett is correct that 80 percent of conversions in frontier territories are linked to some type of charismatic witness, this may be part of the reason for evangelistic success: The vast majority of the world has a supernatural orientation. They want, need and will accept only a gospel that comes with supernatural power.

Power Encounters

The nineties will be a decade rife with supernatural phenomena. In the Western world, our sterile technology has created a thirst for metaphysical experience. Many try to satiate this thirst by flirting with Eastern religions or the occult. Yet this thirst can never be truly satisfied until we come to the One who said, "If anyone thirsts, let him come to Me and drink" (John 7:37). Heaven-initiated experiences of supernatural power are the only effective, Christian counter to the proliferation of unclean, other-worldly phenomena.

As Jesus said in Acts 1:8, the fullness of the Holy Spirit is given for the purpose of effective Christian witness. The eminent expositor D. Martyn Lloyd-Jones saw a direct correlation between the anointing of the Holy Spirit and evangelism. "Go through Acts and in every instance when we are told either that the Spirit came upon these men or that they were filled with the Spirit, you will find that it was in order to bear a witness and a testimony."[1]

In Jesus' ministry and in the ministries of the early Christian disciples, some kind of power encounter often verified their Spirit-anointed gospel proclamation. What is a "power encounter"? C. Peter Wagner, commenting on power encounters among tribal groups, writes that "a power encounter is a visible, practical demonstration that Jesus Christ is more powerful than the false gods or spirits worshiped or feared by a people group." [2] John Wimber adds, "Any system or force that must be overcome for the gospel to be believed is cause for a power encounter." [3]

At a time of acute discouragement, John the Baptist requested reassurance that Jesus was the Messiah. Jesus responded, "Go and tell John the things which you hear and see: The blind receive their sight and the lame walk; the lepers are cleansed and the deaf hear; the dead are raised up and the poor have the gospel preached to them" (Matt. 11:4-5). Jesus saw these miracles, or power encounters, as the verifying credentials of His ministry.

The only New Testament model we have for the ministry of the evangelist is Philip. The report of Philip's evangelistic crusade in Samaria is also a model for biblical evangelism.

> Then Philip went down to the city of Samaria and preached Christ to them.
>
> And the multitudes with one accord heeded the things spoken by Philip, hearing and seeing the miracles which he did.
>
> For unclean spirits, crying with a loud voice, came out of many who were possessed; and many who were paralyzed and lame were healed.
>
> And there was great joy in that city (Acts 8:5-8).

41

Notice that Philip's audience did not just hear; they *heard and saw*. Philip's evangelistic ministry was, first and foremost, preaching Christ. The preaching was augmented, however, by a deliverance ministry and the working of miracles. The Scripture suggests that the people were not convinced of the veracity of Philip's message by his preaching only. They "heeded the things spoken by Philip, hearing and seeing the miracles which he did."

Paul slips his missionary strategy into his letter to the church at Rome.

> For I will not dare to speak of any of those things which Christ has not accomplished through me, in word and deed, to make the Gentiles obedient—in mighty signs and wonders, by the power of the Spirit of God, so that from Jerusalem and round about to Illyricum I have fully preached the gospel of Christ.
>
> And so I have made it my aim to preach the gospel, not where Christ was named, lest I should build on another man's foundation, but as it is written: "To whom He was not announced, they shall see; and those who have not heard shall understand" (Rom. 15:18-21).

Paul's commitment to "frontier evangelism" clearly emerges in this text. He also spotlights three avenues of getting the gospel to the nations: word, deeds and signs and wonders. In missionary strategy, evangelicals have emphasized proclamation (word). The mainline denominations have stressed the social implications of the gospel (deeds). Pentecostals and charismatics have given high profile to signs and wonders. Paul said, in essence, "I employ all three!" A careful, Spirit-orchestrated mix of word, deeds and miracles is the biblical strategy for reaching the nations.

If anyone could have relied on his academic prowess, it was Paul. Paul appeared to take the apologetics approach to evangelism in one place, Athens. There he won the debate with the Greek philosophers but he lost the war; while there was limited evangelistic success, no church was planted.

I do not wish to be misunderstood. There will always be an important place for apologetics evangelism. Throughout his anointed ministry replete with power encounters, Paul went to the synagogues and reasoned with the Jews. Nevertheless, it is probably true both then and now that for every person won to Christ through apologetics, hundreds are won through anointed proclamation and power encounters.

Paul probably kicked himself spiritually all the way from Athens to Corinth. By the time he arrived, he was committed to another style of ministry than what he used in Athens.

> And I, brethren, when I came to you, did not come with excellence of speech or of wisdom declaring to you the testimony of God.
>
> For I determined not to know anything among you except Jesus Christ and Him crucified.
>
> I was with you in weakness, in fear, and in much trembling.
>
> And my speech and my preaching were not

with persuasive words of human wisdom, but in demonstration of the Spirit and of power, that your faith should not be in the wisdom of men but in the power of God (1 Cor. 2:1-5).

The writer of Hebrews also urges readers to give careful attention to their walk with the Lord. "How shall we escape if we ignore such a great salvation? This salvation, which was first announced by the Lord, was confirmed to us by those who heard him. God also testified to it by signs, wonders and various miracles, and gifts of the Holy Spirit distributed according to his will" (Heb. 2:3-4, NIV).

This sampling of New Testament passages gives some indication of the place of power encounters in evangelism. A gospel that shows physical results will produce evangelistic results. T.L. Osborn probably has been used by God in power evangelism as much as any person since the first century. He says, "Whether it is Peter in traditional Jerusalem, Philip in immoral Samaria, or Paul on the pagan island of Melita, the same results always followed; they proclaimed the gospel, miracles were in evidence, and multitudes believed and were added to the church."[4]

Signs and wonders are not meant to be ends in themselves. The purpose of a sign is to point people in a definite direction. The purpose of a supernatural sign is to point people to Jesus Christ. A "wonder" is intended to bring the element of wonder into Christianity. Wonders help guard the Christian faith from degenerating into stale, rationalistic propositions.

Another Look at the Commission

Jesus gave the evangelistic mandate just prior to His ascension. But at creation God gave a cultural mandate. We are under orders to fulfill this mandate as well. God commanded our first parents,

> Be fruitful and multiply; fill the earth and subdue it; have dominion over the fish of the sea, over the birds of the air, and over every living thing that moves on the earth.
> ...See, I have given you every herb that yields seed which is on the face of all the earth, and every tree whose fruit yields seed; to you it shall be for food (Gen. 1:28-29).

One does not have to espouse every tenet of "dominion theology" to understand that God clearly intended for mankind to be in charge. Theologians sometimes speak of man as being the viceroy over God's creation, called to steward the resources of earth on God's behalf.

When sin entered, man began to lose dominion. Millennia have passed since Adam and Eve were expelled from the garden. Now humanity's hold over the rest of the created order seems to be almost neutralized. Consider the fact that an ever-growing portion of humankind is overwhelmed by weeds and chemicals, components of the plant kingdom over which we were to have thorough control. We must further concede that that small component of creation—the atom—could be humankind's undoing. These tragedies are part of the wages of sin.

For many, the gospel of redemption does not begin

with New Testament stories but with humanity's loss of authority in the beginning. Some time ago I was discussing this with T.L. Osborn. He explained to me that his method of evangelistic preaching overseas is to apply to contemporary life a miracle story from the ministry of Jesus. In each message he explains 1) God's good creation; 2) what Satan has done to destroy and pervert God's good creation; and 3) how Jesus has redeemed what the devil sought to destroy.

In other words, charismatics sometimes have a point of entry in gospel preaching that is different from that of evangelicals. Our message does not necessarily begin with the *kerugma*; it often begins with God's creation. The message does not start with redemption; it culminates with redemption. Ours is a message of restoration. Most charismatics believe that, since the cross, God has been "crescendoing" His redemptive and restorative work. "For this purpose the Son of God was manifested, that He might destroy the works of the devil" (1 John 3:8).

"Jesus is Lord" is more than a charismatic slogan. It is a declaration of the present-tense authority of Jesus Christ over every circumstance. Among Pentecostals, charismatics and third-wave participants, the lordship of Christ is foundational and it supersedes any obstacles. While some may allow this confidence to degenerate into fleshly arrogance, when true New Testament power is at work, everything and everybody bows to Jesus. Since most of the world has a supernatural orientation, a gospel with verifying power is better suited to meet felt needs than is a gospel without it. As Peter Wagner states, "Across the board, the most effective evangelism in today's world is accompanied by manifestations of supernatural power." [5]

Another look at the Great Commission reveals that every statement of it is accompanied by a promise of power. In Matthew 28:18-19 before Jesus says, "Go therefore and make disciples of all nations," He says, "All authority is given to Me." In Mark 16:15,17 Jesus commands His disciples to preach the gospel to every person. Then He says, "And these signs will follow those who believe." In Luke 24 He tells His disciples that they will be witnesses of the things they have seen. But first they must "tarry in the city of Jerusalem until you are endued with power from on high" (v. 49). In John 20:21-22 Jesus says to His disciples, "As the Father has sent Me, I also send you." Then immediately He breathed on them and said, "Receive the Holy Spirit." Acts 1:8 is a rebuke to activism without accompanying spiritual power. How motivated the disciples must have been when the resurrected Christ commanded them to evangelize the world! But then He cooled His disciples' heels, in essence saying, "Go...but not yet." Before they became His witnesses, they were to receive power when the Holy Spirit would come on them.

Effective evangelists in any culture must be convinced of four truths. First, they must be convinced of the *power of the gospel*. Paul said, "For I am not ashamed of the gospel of Christ, for it is the power of God to salvation for everyone who believes, for the Jew first and also for the Greek" (Rom. 1:16).

Effective evangelists also trust the *power of the whole*

of Scripture. They know that when they preach the Bible they are preaching the very Word of God. Not only is God's Word cross-cultural; it transcends cultures. The Bible is not judged by the yardstick of any culture. Rather all cultures are judged by the standard of the Bible. " 'Is not My word like fire?' says the Lord, 'and like a hammer that breaks the rock in pieces?' " (Jer. 23:29).

Further, effective evangelists place confidence in the *power of the name of Jesus*. They realize that every knee must bow before His name. When interrogated for the healing of the lame man, Peter replied, "And His name, through faith in His name, has made this man strong, whom you see and know" (Acts 3:16). Jesus is earth's sweetest and strongest name.

Finally, effective evangelists rest in the *power of the Holy Spirit*. They realize that evangelism is a sovereign work. The Holy Spirit is the great evangelist. The best laid plans of men and women are inadequate if the breath of God's life doesn't animate them. Evangelistic effectiveness is " 'not by might nor by power, but by My Spirit,' says the Lord of hosts" (Zech. 4:6).

The power of the Holy Spirit is the definitive edge in effective evangelism. Charles Kraft, professor of anthropology and intercultural communication at Fuller Seminary, addresses this.

> Jesus' kingdom people are to receive the Spirit of the Lord as He did, through the infilling of the Holy Spirit (Lk. 3:21-22). Then in the power and authority given by God, we are like Jesus to release poor, captive, blind, and oppressed

people from the enemy because God values and loves His creatures. For "the time has come" when God will rescue those who have fallen under the evil influence of Satan.

Jesus assumes conflict and enlists us in His war. Then we, like Jesus, are to use *God's power to demonstrate God's love.*[6]

Where We Are

As we endeavor to look toward A.D. 2000, most people see a mixed bag of unprecedented opportunities coupled with the potential for unprecedented clashes of religions and ideologies. One pessimistic analyst, when asked to predict the next decade, replied simply, "Blood." Some estimates suggest that some three hundred thousand people may lose their lives for the testimony of Jesus this year. There seems to be no possibility of penetrating the Muslim world without significant numbers of Christian martyrs.

It appears that every major religion is becoming more militant. A revived Islam is once again aggressively militant in many quarters. Bored with "white magic," the occult has turned brutal. Even Hindus, known historically as pacifists, are now often confrontational. The religion of secular humanism wages its propaganda war in theaters, courtrooms, classrooms and legislatures, often winning. Many Christians are choosing to fight through acts of resistance.

It is indeed true that biblical Christianity is becoming more militant. But our militancy is of a different order. Our war is not with people; it is with demonic spirits who hold people captive. People who oppose Christianity are not the enemy. They are victims of the enemy. Jesus said, "From the days of John the Baptist until now, the kingdom of heaven has been forcefully advancing, and forceful men lay hold of it" (Matt. 11:12, NIV).

All Christian advance is forceful advance. Some existing kingdom has to be displaced to plant the kingdom of God. This requires warfare—spiritual warfare. And, in most areas, it also requires power encounters.

Our weapons are entirely different from those employed by other armies. And no effective counter has yet been found to our weapons! Bombs can be countered with bombs. Rhetoric can be countered with rhetoric. Hate can be countered with hate. But aggressive love— how do you counter that?

The international Christian army, equipped with "God's power to demonstrate God's love," is forcefully advancing worldwide. Africa, south of the Sahara, will be over 50 percent Christian by the turn of the century. Evangelicals in Latin America (most of whom are Pentecostals and charismatics) are experiencing staggering growth. Even amid tragic scandals, America's charismatic churches continue to grow. Singapore, Korea and China have become hot points of the outpouring of the Holy Spirit in Asia. The gospel is advancing in the island nations. Churches in Eastern Europe and in the Soviet Union are breathing fresh breezes of hope and renewal. And "post-Christian" Western Europe is now experiencing isolated brush fires of revival that could become a continental flame.

Missionary giants like William Carey, Hudson Taylor and William Cameron Townsend opened major blocks of humanity to the gospel. Added to the impressive list of evangelical giants are the international ministries of many full-gospel pioneers including Morris Cerullo, Costa Deir, H.B. Garlock, T.L. Osborn, Syvelle Phillips and Lester Sumrall. These courageous trend-setters have helped pave the way for another set of international spiritual generals, including Reinhard Bonnke, Yonggi Cho, Rick Seaward and a host of powerful national leaders.

A People for His Name

The new breed of international Christian leaders will be no strangers to signs and wonders. The science of missiology will continue to play a vital role in the overall scheme of things for world evangelization. However, Spirit-empowered Christians will never be content merely to log what is happening. They must be a part of making it happen! The new breed of church leaders, particularly from the Third World, is demanding a return to a total dependence on the Holy Spirit and a total yieldedness to Him. They, and I, agree with Hudson Taylor's assessment of another generation: "We have given too much attention to methods, and to machinery, and to resources, and too little to the Source of Power, the filling with the Holy Ghost." [7]

When the church is filled with God's power, it becomes a force in the earth. As T.L. Osborn says, the church then becomes "a mighty army whose soldiers of love are to reach every land and plant Christ's banner of salvation in every nation! As ambassadors of the King of kings, the Christian's business is to evangelize every land and 'take out of them a people for His name' (Acts 15:14). This is the purpose of Pentecost."[8]

The Holy Spirit has vouchsafed the still-secret strategies that will unlock all doors hindering world evangelization. John Wimber states, "It is the Holy Spirit, the 'go-between God,' who holds the key to power encounters. Our openness and availability to His direction and enabling, anointing, and power are the catalyst for fulfilling the great commission."[9]

There are other ingredients needed for effective evangelism. They too are supplied by the Holy Spirit. We will discuss one of these in the next chapter.

FOUR

Priority Number One

The world-wide proclamation of the gospel awaits accomplishment by a generation which shall have the obedience, courage and determination to attempt the task. —John R. Mott

A scene from my first trip to India seared my heart. One day I watched helplessly as a young girl, perhaps ten years old, dodged her way across a crowded street. She was obviously malnourished; her protruding stomach contrasted sharply with the rest of her emaciated frame. She carried a large tray piled high with fruit and vegetables. She darted past tons of protected protein—India's sacred cows. Finally, on the other side of the road, she knelt and offered the tray of food at a small shrine—to rot in front of the "hungry" deities. That day I saw clearly that this social evil was not the result of bad economics but bad theology.

For this reason I have little sympathy for some of the ill-informed bleeding hearts of the Western world who view Christian persuaders as villains for challenging the long-established religions of other lands. I make no apologies for being a Christian evangelist. Christianity, by its very nature, is evangelistic. We are on a rescue mission with eternal consequences.

Too often we major in minors while minoring in majors. Christian missions work on several givens—assumptions on which the passion for global evangelism rests. One of the most basic of these assumptions is that people who are without Jesus Christ are lost. I firmly believe that one's emotional involvement in missions will be in direct proportion to the strength of one's belief in the doctrine of the lostness of mankind. The reason for much of our lethargy lies at this point. Though we may give mental assent to this truth, often we do not emotionally come to grips with its consequences.

If people are lost outside of Christ, and if faith in Jesus Christ is the only avenue of redemption, what could possibly be a higher priority than spreading the gospel as far as we can as fast as we can? Anything the church does that is not directly tied to evangelism is not unlike rearranging the furniture while the house is on fire!

Is Humanity Really Lost?

I shall never forget the stabbing words of a Japanese exchange student. "I thought Christianity was important in this country," she said. "But now I know it isn't. After all, I've been here for a year and no one has talked to me about Jesus."

Leighton Ford tells the story of a prison chaplain who tried to share the gospel with a condemned man. After listening to the minister's appeal, the prisoner replied, "Do you really believe what you say, chaplain? If I believed your gospel were true, I would crawl across England on broken glass to tell men about it."[1] Surely the urgency of our witness will measure the reality of our beliefs.

Even in theologically conservative circles, we are battling a new, creeping universalism. Some who are otherwise Bible-believing Christians seem to question the reality of judgment, especially for those who have never heard the gospel. It is not that they have formally removed their belief in hell and judgment. There is simply an eerie silence, even among evangelicals, as many endeavor to sort out in their hearts what they hold to be true.

Universalism, the belief that all people will eventually be saved, is never a friend to warmhearted evangelism. Billy Graham has said, "The various shades of universalism prevalent throughout the church have done more to blunt evangelism and take the heart out of the missionary movement than anything else. I believe the Scriptures teach that men outside of Jesus Christ are lost."[2]

Universalism is an ancient heresy. It began in the Garden of Eden when the serpent told Adam and Eve, "You will not surely die" (Gen. 3:4). One of its first proponents was Origen of Alexandria and it was later condemned by the church. Different shades of the teaching have periodically appeared, noticeably in post-Reformation times, as a reaction to a strict doctrine of election, and in the nineteenth century, when it was sometimes referred to as "the larger hope."

It should be stated at the outset, however, that the character of God is not on trial. Our belief in the Bible is on trial but God's justice is not. The God of all the earth will do right. Any decision He makes regarding those who have not heard will be executed according to His standards of equally perfect righteousness and love.

Neither Scripture nor our historic posture on the subject leaves any doubt as to the final destiny of those without Christ. Scripture clearly describes a coming apocalypse

> when the Lord Jesus is revealed from heaven with His mighty angels, in flaming fire taking vengeance on those who do not know God, and on those who do not obey the gospel of our Lord Jesus Christ.
>
> These shall be punished with everlasting destruction from the presence of the Lord and from the glory of His power (2 Thess. 1:7-9).

Polycarp, one of the early church fathers, faced a vicious martyrdom in a Roman arena with wild beasts. The proconsul urged this aged Christian to renounce his faith in Christ but to no avail. Finally the authority threatened, "I will have you consumed with fire, if you despise wild beasts, unless you change your mind."

Polycarp replied, "You threaten fire which burns for an hour and is soon quenched; for you are ignorant of the fire of the coming judgment and eternal punishment reserved for the wicked." Polycarp, having already given himself up for dead, sought only the salvation of his executioner.[3]

To the testimony of the Scriptures and countless Christian martyrs, the historic creeds of the church add their affirmation of a real heaven and a real hell. One of the great theological documents of history is the Westminster Confession. This statement of faith declares clearly, "...But the wicked, who know not God, and obey not the gospel of Jesus Christ, shall be cast into eternal torments, and be punished with everlasting destruction from the presence of the Lord and the glory of His power."

In more modern times as well evangelical Christians have affirmed the reality not only of a place of eternal blessing but also of a place of eternal torment. The Baptist Faith and Message states, "The unrighteous will be consigned to Hell, the place of everlasting punishment. The righteous in their resurrected and glorified bodies will receive their reward and will dwell forever in Heaven with the Lord." The Statement of Fundamental Truths of the Assemblies of God declares, "Whosoever is not found written in the Book of Life, together with the devil and his angels, the beast and the false prophet, will be consigned to everlasting punishment in the lake which burneth with fire and brimstone, which is the second death."

often quoted verse in the Bible clearly
nity's only two options: perishing or having everlasting life. "For God so loved the world that
He gave His only begotten Son, that whoever believes
in Him should not perish but have everlasting life" (John
3:16). The subsequent verses remind us that God's dis-
position toward humankind is love and forgiveness:
"For God did not send His Son into the world to condemn the world, but that the world through Him might
be saved. He who believes in Him is not condemned;
but he who does not believe is condemned already,
because he has not believed in the name of the only
begotten Son of God" (John 3:17-18).

As Paul thought of his own people being lost, he
wrote, "I have great sorrow and continual grief in my
heart" (Rom. 9:2). He added that he would be willing
to give up his place in Christ and be separated from Him
if by such a sacrifice others would be saved. Paul believed all people outside of Christ were lost, and it left
him with a broken heart.

It is precisely this scandal of an unbroken heart that
impedes evangelism today. The harvest is immense and
ready to be gathered by those who have sown in tears.
"Those who sow in tears shall reap in joy. He who con-
tinually goes forth weeping, bearing seed for sowing,
shall doubtless come again with rejoicing, bringing his
sheaves with him" (Ps. 126:5-6). The crown of rejoicing awaits those who win souls (see 1 Thess. 2:19-20).
"Those who are wise shall shine like the brightness of
the firmament, and those who turn many to righteousness like the stars forever and ever" (Dan. 12:3).

Jesus Christ is Truth incarnate. Truth cannot utter an untruth. He clearly declared that ''no one comes to the Father, except through Me'' (John 14:6).

Jesus spoke often of the terrible place of torment for those who were not reconciled to God. He told the story of an arrogant, wealthy man who, in hell, screamed and pleaded for just a drop of water. The man cried, ''I am tormented in this flame'' (Luke 16:24). Jesus said there would be those who would go ''into the everlasting fire'' (Matt. 25:41) and ''into everlasting punishment'' (Matt. 25:46).

The late W.T. Conner, godly president of South-western Baptist Seminary, once heard two students outside his office flippantly joking about hell. He met the young preachers in the hall, put his arms around their shoulders and escorted them to a large picture window overlooking the city of Fort Worth. As they gazed out the window, the younger men noticed that tears were coursing down Conner's cheeks. ''Don't joke about hell, boys,'' he said softly. ''People are going there. People are going there.''

The destiny of those outside of Christ is no laughing matter. God is not desirous that anyone perish (see 2 Pet. 3:9). We should share the heart of God. Jesus tasted death for every person (see Heb. 2:9). That means the potential of redemption stretches to the entire human race. Look again at Calvary. See God's Son as He hangs on the cross. In history's most awesome moment, He who knew no sin became sin for us (2 Cor. 5:21). Your sins, my sins, the sins of the entire world were in that moment smashed on Him. The literal meaning of Isaiah

53:6 is "the Lord has caused to land on Him the iniquity of us all." Jesus Christ was separated from the Father so that we might never need to be separated. Jesus, being infinite, suffered in a finite period what we, being finite, would have suffered for an infinite period of time.

What If They Haven't Heard?

A young person came to me not long ago with a troubled look on his face. "I love the Lord and I believe the Bible," he told me. "But I just can't believe that God would condemn someone who has never heard the gospel." Let's face squarely this difficult question. What if they haven't heard?

In the first chapter of Romans Paul makes an excellent case for the lostness of humanity. He reminds us that men and women are not only going to be lost when they die. They are born in sin as descendants of Adam and inherently separated from God. The Bible says the unbelieving person is "condemned already" and that "the wrath of God abides on him" (John 3:18,36). Paul gives an airtight argument that every person stands accountable to God because of the light of conscience and the testimony of God in creation.

This testimony of nature is sometimes called general revelation. Creation's general revelation of God powerfully preaches a person's accountability to his or her Creator. However, only the specific revelation of God in Jesus Christ shows how we can be justified before this holy Creator-God. According to Paul, even the remotest of people are "without excuse" because of the light of conscience and nature. Yet only the light of the world, Jesus Christ, can bring them salvation.

It is important to understand that rejection of the gospel is not the only criterion for lostness. Humanity is already lost because of sin. That blankets all people everywhere. "For all have sinned and fall short of the glory of God" (Rom. 3:23). We are sinners because of the wrongs we have done. But we are also sinners because of who we are—children of Adam. As his offspring, we are born with a proclivity to sin. The issue is not a question: Has light come to us? The issue is a statement: Humanity is already in darkness.

A word of warning needs to be added here. Those of us who live in nations historically blessed with the gospel have had the privilege of a brighter light. Individual Christians, churches and media have drenched this country with the good news. God's Word makes clear that the greater the light rejected, the greater the condemnation. I believe the Bible teaches that many so-called "Christian nations" will face a judgment stiffer than that of other nations. "Of how much worse punishment, do you suppose, will he be thought worthy who has trampled the Son of God underfoot, counted the blood of the covenant by which he was sanctified a common thing, and insulted the Spirit of grace?" (Heb. 10:29).

When they stand before God most Americans will not be asked, What about the people who haven't heard? The question will be, What about you? You *have* heard.

Again it needs to be stated that God's character is not on trial. He can be trusted to do what is completely just and right. When we ponder His mercy, this whole issue is flipped. Since God is perfectly holy, the wonder is not that some will be lost. The great wonder is that anyone from rebellious humanity is saved!

God has gone to the very limits of boundless love to prevent humankind from perishing. God incarnate became sin incarnate on the cross! It is too much to fathom fully. Yet it is wonderfully true. As we moved toward judgment, God intervened personally through Christ. "He is the atoning sacrifice for our sins, and not only for ours but also for the sins of the whole world" (1 John 2:2, NIV).

The question of the lostness of those who have not heard the gospel is a vital issue. It must be resolved in one's heart (at least by faith) before missionary passion can flow in fullness. While the question is usually raised in utmost sincerity, the one who doubts the lostness of those who haven't heard should carry that argument to its logical conclusion. If those who haven't heard are not accountable, we should immediately rush every missionary home and prevent every national worker from reaching any further. After all, what if those previously unaccountable were to hear the gospel and reject it? They would then be accountable. The missionary would have done them a terrible disservice. Such a line of reasoning would have to conclude that the kindest thing we could do for yet unreached humanity would be to stop preaching the gospel! It is little wonder that such reasoning dwarfs missionary advance.

But in fact those who have not heard the gospel are just as lost as those who have heard and rejected it.

Therefore, the most benevolent, humanitarian activity in the world is preaching the gospel. The benefits of reception of the message begin immediately. Time and again, social transformation has resulted from the infiltration of the gospel into a society. But the benefits are also eternal. Those who hear and obey the gospel now possess eternal life. Dick Hillis, founder of Overseas Crusades, brings the issue to a verdict:

> If those who have not heard will somehow be saved, would it not then be best if they did not hear?
>
> Did Christ misguide His followers when He sent Paul throughout all Asia Minor and Europe? Or when He sent William Carey to India, Hudson Taylor to China, and tens of thousands of missionaries around the world?
>
> If the unevangelized are not lost, is not the mission program of the church a ludicrous blunder? Are millions of dollars spent on a useless program? Are thousands of man hours wasted by missionaries? If the unreached are not lost, does not the Scripture become a bundle of contradictions, the Savior become a false teacher, the Christian message become "much ado about nothing"? [4]

Carey
Taylor

All evidence points in the other direction. Most of the adherents of the world's great religions are sincere. Yet sincerity is not what saves us. Only faith in the finished work of Jesus Christ brings salvation. Holy Scripture does not suggest any alternative plan. We have

→ 지성이면 감천이다 " NOT so

a distinct message—the only message that can set humanity's captives free. As someone has said, "The gospel is not a message that we would invent if we could nor one we could invent if we would." The Christian message does not parrot other religions. Our faith is gloriously unique.

"We Have to Go Out"

In light of His sacrifice, we must go, endued with the Spirit's power to actualize that for which Christ died. It was this motivation that spurred Nikolaus von Zinzendorf and the Moravian missionaries "to win for the Lamb all those whom His blood has purchased." Paul, that great missionary, cried, "...necessity is laid upon me; yes, woe is me if I do not preach the gospel!" (1 Cor. 9:16). John Knox pled on his knees, "Give me Scotland or I die." Hudson Taylor, as a young man in England, cried to God, "I feel that I cannot go on living unless I do something for China." Robert Arthington could not go overseas but, through sacrifice, helped send others. He lived in a single room, cooked his own meals and gave over $500,000 to missions. At the end of his life he wrote, "Gladly would I again make the floor my bed, a box my chair, another box my table, rather than that men should perish for want of the knowledge of the Savior."

Each of these men had a heart pumping with what Oswald J. Smith called "a passion for souls." Do you have that passion? Do you long for more? The believer who is intimate with the Holy Spirit is advantaged here. Why? "Because the love of God has been poured out in our hearts by the Holy Spirit'' (Rom. 5:5).

Late one night a concerned lighthouse keeper watched as a violent storm erupted at sea. Suddenly the seasoned keeper saw the faint SOS of a ship in distress. Grabbing his raincoat, he looked at his young apprentice and commanded, ''Let's go!''

Horrified, the apprentice retorted, ''But, sir, if we go out there, we may never come back.''

The old keeper of the lighthouse paused and put his hand on the young man's shoulder. "Son," he responded, "we have to go out. We don't have to come back."

No one doubts that there is great peril in penetrating the final frontiers. But that is not the issue. What matters is that people are perishing. We have to go out. We don't have to come back. The global Christian advance is a rescue operation. 구원의 사역

The great gospel songwriter Fanny Crosby was asked which of her thousands of lyrics she considered her best. After pondering the question, that blind saint replied, ''I think it's this one'':

> Down in the human heart, crushed by the
>   tempter,
> Feelings lie buried that grace can restore;
> Touched by a loving heart, wakened by
>   kindness,
> Chords that are broken will vibrate once more.
>
> Rescue the perishing, care for the dying;
> Jesus is merciful, Jesus will save.

FIVE

Let's Pray the Global Harvest In

Prayer is the one mission to the world that all Christians can share. Through prayer any of us can directly love the unreached, even to the ends of the earth. As far as God can go, prayer can go. —*David Bryant*

Some time ago I sat in the parlor of the administration building of the Bible College of Wales, taking a proper British tea with Samuel Howells. In hushed, courteous tones I discussed with this deeply spiritual man what God is doing in the world today. Warm sun bathed the room through the leaded glass windows. The only interruption in the tranquility was the occasional chirping of birds in the large oak trees outside.

It was hard to imagine that this serene spot, nestled away in the Welsh countryside, was one of the most important nerve centers of global activity in World War II. From this place Rees Howells and his faithful staff waged war in the heavenlies against evil principalities and powers. By the sheer strength of prayer they helped force the retreat and final defeat of Hitler's mighty, satanic war machine.[1]

Lord Tennyson was right. "More things are wrought by prayer than this world dreams of."

Now, a half century later, the church is engaged in a warfare no less real and no less deadly. The denizens of hell and the army of the Lord Jesus Christ are locked in a battle for the minds and souls of this generation. The death, resurrection and ascension of our mighty Lord assure us of ultimate victory. The key to actualizing the victory already purchased is to engage in massive streams of intercession.

Paul Billheimer said,

> The praying people are the body politic of the world, and the church holds the balance of power in world affairs. Not only in future ages is she the ruling and governing force in the social order, but even now, in this present throbbing moment, by means of her prayer power and to the extent to which she uses it, the praying church is actually deciding the course of human events. Some day we shall discover that prayer is the most important factor in shaping the course of human history.[2]

Dick Eastman says, "I am convinced that when we stand before God...we will discover that *every* soul ever brought to a knowledge of Christ was in some way related to intercessory prayer."[3] I too am convinced that, above all other factors, effectual prayer is our most potent key for world evangelization. It makes everything else we do in missions possible. A noted missions authority has said that all progress in missions is directly related to prayer. It has prepared the way for each new triumph and has been the key to all success.

Who Controls the Harvest?

All signs point to a global harvest of staggering, unprecedented proportions. For churches that will wage the war and garner the harvest, there will be colossal growth. As God's loving heart gathers in this generation, we will come to expect churches of ten-thousand-plus dotting the landscape of cities around the world.

Yet many Christians have been so beaten down that they find it difficult to believe God for such a harvest. I am amazed at how many Christians act as though Satan, not Jesus, were the lord of the harvest. While we would never actually say it, many Christians live as though Satan has the keys to hell and death. Whether or not the devil ever had the keys may be debatable, but one thing is certain: He doesn't have them now! Jesus declared, "I am He who lives, and was dead, and behold, I am alive forevermore. Amen. And I have the keys of Hades and of Death" (Rev. 1:18).

Although the devil is the prince and power of the air, this planet does not belong to him. The earth and its inhabitants by judicial right belong to God. "The earth is the Lord's, and all its fullness, the world and those who dwell therein'' (Ps. 24:1). When Jesus purchased redemption, the potential of that sacrifice stretched to the entire human race. Scripture declares that He, by the grace of God, tasted death for everyone (see Heb. 2:9). Consequently we can pray with bold expectancy for an immense harvest, realizing that by every right humanity does not belong to Satan but to Jesus.

Then there are believers who, though they realize that the devil is not in ultimate control, believe that somehow they themselves are the arbiters of the harvest. Many of us have fallen into this trap at times. We have sat around conference tables brainstorming about evangelism—as if we could make the harvest happen. We're drowning in charts, graphs and feasibility studies on how best to evangelize the world. Yet the world remains lost!

If smart ideas could get the job done, then our seminaries should be lighthouses of evangelistic genius, with no unevangelized people for miles around. I am not throwing stones at seminaries or churches. I'm simply saying that, while missiological data is undoubtedly helpful, good ideas don't produce harvest. There have been some seven hundred plans for world evangelization. But not one has yet succeeded fully.

No, Satan is not in charge of the harvest. Neither are we. *Jesus* is the Lord of the harvest. Jesus reminded us, ''The harvest truly is plentiful, but the laborers are few. Therefore pray the Lord of the harvest to send out laborers into *His* harvest'' (Matt. 9:37-38). Let's get it straight: We're not the ones who produce the harvest; we are laborers in the harvest. Whose harvest is it? It is His harvest. Jesus is the arbiter of the harvest.

If Jesus is in control of the harvest, then the natural question is, how large does He want His harvest to be? The answer is clear. He is "not willing that *any* should perish but that all should come to repentance" (2 Pet. 3:9). Therefore, when we pray to the Lord of the harvest, we pray for His will to be done in relation to the harvest. His desire is that everyone experience His salvation and lordship. Why, then, are not all saved? Because they have not all repented and turned to Christ. Why have they not come to Him? Because we have not cared enough to rescue by prayer these spiritual POWs out of the kingdom of darkness and into the kingdom of light.

Andrew Murray said,

> There is a world, with its needs entirely dependent on and waiting to be helped by intercession; there is a God in heaven, with His all-sufficient supply for all those needs, waiting to be asked; there is a Church, with its wondrous calling and its sure promises, waiting to be roused to a sense of its wondrous responsibility and power.[4]

The Theater of War

In Ephesians 6 Paul speaks of an elaborate armor for believers. Thankfully, we are hearing more teaching on this timely subject of putting on the armor of God. Tragically, however, many Christians who put on the armor never show up for the war! After Paul details the pieces of the armor, he gives a battle call for us to

71

be "praying always with all prayer and supplication in the Spirit, being watchful to this end with all perseverance and supplication for all the saints" (Eph. 6:18). He goes on to request prayer for boldness and an open door for the preaching of the gospel.

In the violent student protests of the 1960s several antiwar slogans surfaced. One of the slogans arrested the nation's attention: "What if they gave a war and nobody came?"

While the protesters intended this to prod us to rethink our participation in physical combat, the Christian needs to ask the same question in terms of spiritual combat: What if they gave a war and nobody came?

Paul makes it abundantly clear in several of his letters that Christians are engaged in a conflict of cosmic proportions. He describes it in many ways: light against darkness, life against death, the Spirit against the flesh, Christ against Satan.

The apostle assures us of a divine arsenal whereby we can be victorious over Satan's cunning war tactics. Yet this master deceiver has even fooled most Christians as to the correct theater of war. While legitimate political involvement is commendable, the true battleground is not in the Congress but in the closet! The warfare is in the heavens—God's angels and Satan's demons pitted in a death-struggle of global proportions for the minds and souls of men and women. Entire nations are at stake. The believers' weaponry to wrest these nations out of the kingdom of darkness and into the kingdom of light is intercessory prayer. Notice what Paul says in 2 Corinthians 10:3-5:

For though we walk in the flesh, we do not war according to the flesh.

For the weapons of our warfare are not carnal but mighty in God for pulling down strongholds, casting down arguments and every high thing that exalts itself against the knowledge of God, bringing every thought into captivity to the obedience of Christ.

Ralph Mahoney, founder of World MAP, tells the intriguing story of how prayer made the difference in a small rural town situated on the Uruguay-Brazil border. Actually, the national boundary ran down the main street of this town. One morning when a missionary began distributing tracts on the Uruguayan side of the street, he was strongly resisted.

Discouraged, he crossed over to the Brazilian side of the street. Much to his surprise, the people willingly accepted the literature. Some even stopped to read it on the spot. Then the missionary noticed that a woman who had refused a tract on the Uruguayan side crossed ov r to window shop on the Brazilian side. As she approached him he offered her the tract again. She smiled, took the tract and thanked him. He tested several others and many followed the same pattern.

Later as he was praying about these differences, the words of Jesus came to his mind: "No one can enter a strong man's house and plunder his goods, unless he first binds the strong man, and then he will plunder his house" (Mark 3:27). Further investigation suggested a prayer band of Brazilian Christians had been binding the "strong man" over their region. That particular territorial demon-power had been immobilized.

We are often too passive and peaceful in our praying. Read what S.D. Gordon said:

> The greatest agency put into man's hands is prayer. And to define prayer one must use the language of war. Peace language is not equal to the situation. The earth is in a state of war and is being hotly besieged. Thus one must use war talk to grasp the fact with which prayer is concerned.
>
> Prayer from God's side is communication between himself and his allies in enemy country. True prayer moves in a circle. It begins with the heart of God and sweeps down into the human heart, so intersecting the circle of earth, which is the battlefield of prayer, and then goes back again to its starting point, having accomplished its purpose on the downward swing.[5]

Have you ever noticed how Paul tied prayer and evangelism together in 1 Timothy 2:1-4?

> Therefore I exhort first of all that supplications, prayers, intercessions, and giving of thanks be made for all men, for kings and all who are in authority, that we may lead a quiet and peaceable life in all godliness and reverence.
>
> For this is good and acceptable in the sight of God our Savior, who desires all men to be saved and to come to the knowledge of the truth.

When we pray for harvest, we are to pray for the

nations of the world and their leaders. We pray for a peaceful climate that is conducive for evangelistic activity.

Unfortunately, Christians sometimes pray for judgment on nations, thinking that catastrophe will bring people to God. This is seldom true. Europe is only now beginning to recover from the spiritual aftermath of World War II. True, calamity sometimes softens the hearts of people. But often disaster hardens hearts. If war and catastrophe bring people to God, Europe should be one of the most godly places on earth. According to the Bible, it is the goodness of God that leads people to repentance (see Rom. 2:4).

I am convinced that no one is saved except in answer to someone's prayer. That is why we must come against the spiritual darkness that has blinded unbelievers. "But even if our gospel is veiled, it is veiled to those who are perishing, whose minds the god of this age has blinded, who do not believe, lest the light of the gospel of the glory of Christ, who is the image of God, should shine on them" (2 Cor. 4:3-4). We have the authority to strip the veil away and let the light of the gospel shine.

Ask of Me

In recent years God has been raising up a vast army of international intercessors. This burgeoning prayer movement has gathered strong momentum worldwide. Here in America God has used Vonette Bright, David Bryant, Evelyn Christensen, Wesley Duewel, Dick Eastman, Larry Lea, Glenn Sheppard, Bob Willhite and others to summon God's troops to the battlefields of prayer. Each of the people just mentioned has marshalled a cadre of people for intercession. This can only signal glorious impending harvest.

Before his recent death, J. Edwin Orr, one of this century's greatest scholars on spiritual awakening, declared, "I have researched prayer movements in relationship to spiritual awakening for more than half a century. It has drawn me to two conclusions: First, no great spiritual awakening in history ever occurred apart from united prayer. Secondly, after visiting more than 150 countries for over fifty years, I have never heard of or read about a greater united movement of prayer than is now emerging around the world." [6]

It has been my high privilege to participate in the emergence of one stream of the great prayer army. My pastor, Larry Lea, is being used of God to amass an army of three hundred thousand intercessors in North America. When that prayer army is formed, I believe God will use us to tear down strongholds around the world.

At Church on the Rock we have seen the awesome effects of prayer. We are preparing to enter our second decade of daily, early morning prayer meetings. Since 1980 we have met on weekdays at 6:00 a.m. for prayer. Some have come at five. This prayer time has produced the spiritual dynamic for all our evangelistic outreach. For there, at our daily prayer meeting, we bind the demon spirits that hinder the harvest; we loose the Holy Spirit to draw the lost to Christ; we beseech the Lord of the harvest to send forth laborers; we dispatch holy angels to battle the forces of Satan and bring people to

Christ. Can angels do that? That is exactly what they are called to do, according to Hebrews 1:14. Angels are "ministering spirits sent forth to minister to those who will inherit salvation."

We stand on the promise of harvest in Isaiah 43:5-7:

Fear not, for I am with you;
I will bring your descendants from the east,
And gather you from the west;
I will say to the north, "Give them up!"
And to the south,
"Do not keep them back!"
Bring My sons from afar,
And My daughters from the ends of the earth—
Everyone who is called by My name,
Whom I have created for My glory;
I have formed him, yes, I have made him.

We command the evil spirits from each region to give up the harvest that rightfully belongs to God.

This is what God urges us to do in the passage I have chosen as my life verse, Psalm 2:8: "Ask of Me, and I will give You the nations for Your inheritance, and the ends of the earth for Your possession."

An exposition of this passage shows that God the Father is addressing His Son, as the Father anticipates the time when His Son will rule over the nations. Since we are in Christ, and since His rule over the nations has become priority number one for us, we too can ask of Him.

After my father died, I walked through the stabbing grief. One day I was complaining to the Lord that, on top of losing a wonderful father, his finances (and commitments to missions) had been such that he had not left a substantial monetary inheritance.

Lovingly, the Lord spoke back to my heart, "Son, what do you *want* for an inheritance?"

Immediately my heart responded, "Lord, give me nations for my inheritance!"

I believe that experience, when I was sixteen, helped launch many of the privileges of international ministry I enjoy today. Years later, the Lord personalized a promise of Scripture as I was praying for nations. In that divine moment the promise became mine: "I will speak of Your testimonies also before kings, and will not be ashamed" (Ps. 119:46).

Although I accepted this prospect by faith, prayer has made it a reality. I have stood before kings and preached the gospel. I have been the guest of ambassadors and government officials. Recently it was my privilege to pray with the president and the secretary of foreign affairs of an African nation.

These are not coincidences. They are direct answers to claiming God's promise in prayer. Wonderful things— supernatural things—happen when we pray.

We have not yet rallied the full prayer force of the entire church. Just think what would happen if all Christians focused their prayers in the same direction! Nothing could stop that kind of explosive spiritual strength.

Remember what happened when only a small percentage of Christians around the world began praying against Idi Amin's reign of terror in Uganda. In a few months, that tyrant was toppled from power. For years, Christians in the West have prayed for persecuted brothers and sisters behind the Iron Curtain. Now *glasnost* is at least bringing temporary new liberties to the church. Since we Americans are such pragmatists, we ought to warm to prayer. Why? Because, plainly and simply, prayer works.

Of course, this is how the largest church in the world, the Yoido Full Gospel Church of Seoul, has been built. Pastor Paul Yonggi Cho counsels us:

> We have learned that we are at war against Satan in this earth. Our opposition is the devil and his demonic spirits. Our battlefield is the hearts of all men and women. Our goal is that all may come to know the saving grace of our Lord and Savior, Jesus Christ. Therefore, we plan carefully: we have a strategy, we have a plan and we execute that plan like a well-trained army. Yet most importantly, we bathe His breath of life into our efforts and they will be fruitful.
>
> I have not followed a secret formula in the mighty church growth we are experiencing. What I have done is simply take the Word of God seriously. There is no question in my mind that what has been done in Korea can also be duplicated in every part of the world. The key is prayer![7]

I will never forget the thrill of preaching at an all-night prayer meeting at that great Korean church. At 11:00 p.m. the auditorium was jammed with more than ten thousand praying Christians. No wonder they are influencing their nation for Christ.

The Lord's Missionary Prayer

In recent years much attention has been given to what we term the Lord's prayer. Larry Lea's book and tape series *Could You Not Tarry One Hour?* have inspired hundreds of thousands. Lea contends that the Lord provided this prayer as a model track for intercession. Each phrase of the prayer becomes something of a springboard to launch the prayer into greater depths of intercession.

I am one of thousands who testify to a revitalized prayer life following the prayer model of Jesus in Matthew 6. I've been a part of Church on the Rock for nine years, and, as a church, we have studied and restudied this passage. Yet each time it yields new treasures. Such is the wonder of God's Word.

There is great value in dissecting the intricacies of the prayer. But it is also important to see it at face value. When we do, we quickly discover that *the Lord's prayer is a missionary prayer*. Let's look at it again.

"Our Father in heaven, hallowed be Your name." This is the *focus of missions*. World evangelization has its vertex in a God who desires to be known by all humanity as Father. Notice too the careful structure of the sentence. Although this may seem technical, it is important. The Holy Spirit is precise. Although it would be good to pray, "We hallow Your name," this is not what the Lord said. Rather He taught us to pray, "Hallowed be Your name." What's the difference? The

latter is a petition that the name of God be hallowed in those regions where it is not. This phrase is not only a statement of praise. It is a petition with a missionary focus.

"Your kingdom come. Your will be done on earth as it is in heaven." Of course this is the *goal of missions*. This phrase is a poetic couplet, common in Hebrew writing. It is a double statement of a single idea. When His kingdom comes in its fullness, His benevolent fiats will saturate the earth. His will being fully enacted on earth will be the evidence that His kingdom has settled on earth. The verbs appear in the imperative mood in the original language. This is astonishing. This is not to be a weak, fearful plea. Jesus is teaching us to command that God's kingdom, already enforced throughout the rest of the universe, come now on the earth! We are to pray from the general to the specific. When I make this statement, I declare His lordship over the entire earth, reaching ultimately to me.

"Give us this day our daily bread." This is the first of four petitions, sandwiched between the declarations of His rule which begin and finish the prayer. In this prayer, we petition the Lord to give us, forgive us, lead us and deliver us. In praying, "Give us this day our daily bread," we are praying for the *financing of missions*. One of the great impediments to gospel advancement is the lack of necessary funds. We are to look daily to God for the needed supply—and we will need billions of dollars to finish the task. Here we are praying for the *financial ability* to accomplish His stated will.

"And forgive us our debts, as we forgive our debtors."

The emphasis now shifts to the great *problem of missions*: unforgiveness. Amy Carmichael served Christ in India for fifty years without a furlough. She never heard the term *culture shock*. There was another shock, however, that was equally traumatic for this saintly woman. Upon arriving on the mission field, she was shocked to find that missionaries did not love one another. Today as well, efforts are often stymied by our refusal to forgive. This unforgiveness brings serious consequences. Commenting on this portion of the prayer, Jesus said, "For if you forgive men their trespasses, your heavenly Father will also forgive you. But if you do not forgive men their trespasses, neither will your Father forgive your trespasses" (Matt. 6:14-15). It doesn't take a Bible college degree to understand what He meant. This is a prayer for *emotional liberty* and freedom from the chains that come from being unforgiven and/or unforgiving.

"And do not lead us into temptation, but deliver us from the evil one." Here Jesus spotlights the *warfare of missions*. We are to be free personally from the devil's temptations. Thus liberated, we become liberators. As the Bible commands, we "put on the Lord Jesus Christ, and make no provision for the flesh, to fulfill its lusts" (Rom. 13:14). We trust our Shepherd to lead us into pleasant, nurturing pastures. And as He leads us, we will lead others. Because He leads us, we develop *mental maturity*. Since He delivers us, we experience *spiritual authority*.

"For Yours is the kingdom and the power and the glory forever. Amen." As the prayer concludes, Jesus

encourages us with the *finishing of missions*. This *is* the kingdom, the power and the glory. Yes, His kingdom is coming. But it has come already in our hearts. One day the hope of His kingdom will be a reality worldwide. The earth will be filled with the glory of the Lord. But even now our hearts are filled with His glory.

Perhaps you now view this model prayer from a new perspective. If so, I urge you to employ the Lord's missionary prayer as a powerful tool of intercession for a needy world.

Releasing the Global Harvest

As we pray for the release of the harvest, we should remember several things.

First, we should pray *committedly*. In other words, we should have a set time for prayer *and* a spirit of worship and intercession throughout the day. Remember that Peter and John went up together to the temple at the set hour of prayer (see Acts 3:1).

Second, we should pray *fervently*. It is those who pray violently who press into kingdom possibilities. As Jack Hayford says, "Prayer is invading the impossible." Remember, "the effective, fervent prayer of a righteous man avails much" (James 5:16).

Third, we should pray *specifically*. We are to ask in faith for those we want to see come to Christ. Did you ever stop to think that you can wield a sceptre of life or death by your prayers? Jesus gave us a colossal promise, "And I will give you the keys of the kingdom of heaven, and whatever you bind on earth will be bound in heaven, and whatever you loose on earth will be loosed in heaven'' (Matt. 16:19).

Fourth, we should pray *unitedly*. This was one of the real keys to the effectiveness of the early church. When confronted with persecution, ''they raised their voice to God with one accord'' (Acts 4:24). J. Edwin Orr said that it takes ''united, extraordinary prayer'' to see revival. When revival comes, heightened missions activity is the natural result.

Fifth, we should pray *persistently*. Jesus taught that persistence in prayer will yield results. I've heard that George Mueller prayed for fifty-three years for a friend to be converted. The day came when Mueller's friend came to Christ. It did not come until Mueller's casket was lowered in the ground. There, near the open grave, this friend surrendered his heart to the Lord. Persistence had paid off! ''And I say to you, ask, and it will be given to you; seek, and you will find; knock, and it will be opened to you'' (Luke 11:9).

Sixth, we should pray *boldly*. We know that it is God's will to save the lost. ''Let us therefore come boldly to the throne of grace, that we may obtain mercy and find grace to help in time of need'' (Heb. 4:16). Ole Hallesby said, ''Nothing makes us so bold in prayer as when we can look into the eye of God and say to Him, 'Thou knowest that I am not praying for personal advantage, nor to avoid hardship, nor that my own will in any way should be done, but only for this, that Thy name might be glorified.' ''[8] Surely we can say that to God regarding missions.

Finally, we should pray *expectantly*. ''Now this is the confidence that we have in Him, that if we ask anything according to His will, He hears us. And if we know that He hears us, whatever we ask, we know that we have the petitions that we have asked of Him'' (1 John 5:14-15).

A New Era of Intercessors

In 1806 a group of students at Williams College in Massachusetts sought refuge from a sudden rainstorm in a haystack. As the rain beat down, they turned their retreat into a prayer meeting. They asked God to use their lives. As they prayed, their faith rose to believe God could use them significantly to fulfill Christ's Great Commission. When the rain subsided, they left with the rallying cry, ''We can do it if we will!'' This unobtrusive meeting went down in history as the Haystack Prayer Meeting. Today this spontaneous prayer time is seen as the beginning of the mission movement in America. As a result, the American Board of Commissioners for Foreign Missions was birthed.

It was a season of prayer—the Haystack Prayer Meeting—that launched the world missions endeavor in America. Now, as beautiful concerts of prayer rise to the throne from believers in every nation, we will see Satan's fortresses toppled and the kingdom of God established.

At the recent Lausanne International Congress on World Evangelization in Manila, intercessors from many nations prayed around the clock throughout the entire congress for success for the gospel. Surely we may anticipate a massive global surge for the church.

The massive global harvest has already begun! But

who are the gatherers, and who will have the joy of bringing in the harvest? God today always seeks for someone who will make up the hedge and stand in the gap before Him. For such a person, God will go to the limits of this planet to reveal Himself as the wonder-working almighty God. "For the eyes of the Lord run to and fro throughout the whole earth, to show Himself strong on behalf of those whose heart is loyal to Him" (2 Chr. 16:9).

So believe God for the harvest. A new wave of harvest is coming in. A new era is dawning. As E.M. Bounds said,

> We put it as our most sober judgment that the great need of the church in this and all ages is men of such commanding faith, of such unsullied holiness, of such marked spiritual vigor and consuming zeal, that their prayers, faith, lives and ministries will be of such a radical and aggressive form as to work spiritual revolutions which will form eras in individual and church life.[9]

SIX

The Renaissance of World Missions

As long as there are millions destitute of the Word of God and knowledge of Jesus Christ, it will be impossible for me to devote my time and energy to those who have both.
— *J.L. Ewen*

Some years back two rather skeptical clergymen sat on the platform of a Billy Graham crusade. One of them said to the other, "Why doesn't somebody tell this guy Graham that the day of mass evangelism is over?"

Waving his hand across the overflowing stadium, his friend replied, "Why doesn't somebody tell all these people?"

There was also a time, not so long ago, when several were prophesying the doom of world missions. The only problem was they forgot to tell a lot of people—and God.

Still, the crisis of missions decline was real. The 1960s had taken their toll on the church and its mission. Radical theologians were announcing that God was dead.

The Student Volunteer Movement in the early decades of this century had been responsible for some twenty thousand college students' becoming missionaries. Unfortunately, that movement waned as the deadening effects of liberalism dampened their evangelistic fervor. They eventually voted themselves out of existence after concluding that the organization no longer had a message.

As the SVM started to decline, Inter-Varsity Christian Fellowship picked up the slack. In 1946 they began hosting trienniel student missionary conventions, known as the Urbana conventions because they are held on the campus of the University of Illinois at Urbana.

In the sixties the Urbana conventions began to lean toward a political agenda considerably left of center. America was weary of nightly doses of Vietnam and was in no mood for more stories from overseas. Across the world, surging tides of nationalism overturned the worn-out dogmas of imperialism. Amid the cries of "Yankee, go home!" one could often hear, "Missionary, go home!"

It was undeniable that the mainline Protestant denominations for the most part had been lost to liberalism. Evangelicals were reassessing their missions commitments. And the charismatic movement, still in its euphoric formative years, had not yet adopted a missions posture.

But quietly, behind the scenes and behind the headlines, God was at work.

The Premature Funeral of World Missions

Mark Twain once said, "The reports of my death are greatly exaggerated." So were the reports of the demise of missions. In many ways world missions today is healthier than ever. The last few Urbana conventions have drawn some seventeen thousand young people to pray and allow God to call them, if He so chooses, to a career in missions.

Some may think of the days of David Livingstone and Hudson Taylor as the zenith of missions. Yet in Livingstone's day most Christianity in Africa was confined to coastal areas. Today it permeates the continent. Only in Taylor's wildest dreams could he hope for eighty million believers in China. Yet that is the case today. Kenneth Scott Latourette, the imminent historian, called the nineteenth century "the great century" of missions. Yet only in this century has Christianity become a truly global faith, with Christians in every nation on earth.

It may have looked as if missions was beating a retreat in the sixties and early seventies. In fact, God was working in almost imperceptible ways for a massive missions surge. While other events grabbed the headlines, men and movements were being positioned that would shape the future of the church.

In 1966 the World Congress on Evangelism convened in Berlin under the auspices of *Christianity Today* magazine with the assistance of the Billy Graham Evangelistic Association. This gathering of church leaders from around the world signalled an important demarcation from the often leftist-leaning World Council of Churches. Whereas the 1910 World Missionary Conference in Edinburgh failed to produce an adequate definition for evangelism, a very clear statement rang out from the participants in Berlin.

> Evangelism is the proclamation of the Gospel of the crucified and risen Christ, the only Redeemer of men, according to the Scriptures, with the purpose of persuading condemned and lost sinners to put their trust in God by receiving and accepting Christ as Savior through the power of the Holy Spirit, and to serve Christ as Lord in every calling of life and in the fellowship of his Church, looking toward the day of his coming.[1]

Once again Bible-believing Christians worldwide rallied around a crisp statement regarding the church's evangelistic task. The Berlin congress laid a groundwork for the Lausanne International Congresses on World Evangelization in 1974 and 1989.

In 1965 an aging radio evangelist saw the fulfillment of a long-held dream. Charles E. Fuller's "Old Fashioned Revival Hour" broadcast was one of the largest media missions ministries of the 1940s and 1950s. To this day, no one has surpassed the tender pathos Fuller possessed in issuing the appeal to receive Christ. As he grew older, two concerns gripped his heart: the future leadership of the church and the fulfillment of the Great Commission. The founding of

Fuller Theological Seminary was his contribution to the training of leadership. The seminary's School of World Mission, opened in 1965, has become Fuller's lasting contribution to world evangelization.

In another quarter, an equally significant event was occurring in Christian education. Charismatics did not have a major university. Oral Roberts University was founded in 1963 to meet that need. A trans-evangelical breakthrough occurred when Billy Graham gave the keynote address at the investiture of Oral Roberts as the president of the university. In the address, Graham charged the new institution to be ever-faithful to its purpose of promoting world evangelism. Charismatic Bible colleges also began to proliferate in the sixties and seventies, including the far-reaching Christ for the Nations Institute in Dallas.

Around the same time a young Assemblies of God youth pastor was coming to terms with a major discovery. He saw the youth of the church as perhaps the greatest untapped resource for missions. He also saw that mission agencies at the time were ill-equipped to give these young people significant, short-term missions experiences. In response, Loren Cunningham founded Youth With a Mission. Today, YWAM deploys more people for overseas missions service than any other ministry.

In that same time frame, another Assemblies of God youth pastor took some serious-minded Southern California teenagers on a prayer retreat. The weekend became a sacred event as the Lord powerfully assured the interceding young people that their agonizing prayers for their friends had been heard. Within six months of Dick Eastman's prayer retreat, the Jesus movement was sweeping thousands into the kingdom. Many of these young people were committed to a radical life-style before they came to Christ. It was natural for them to continue to be radical—only now it was for Christ and His kingdom. This commitment led them quite easily into missions involvement. Many found their way into YWAM, Campus Crusade for Christ and Teen Challenge works around the world.

Internationally, God was also at work in the nationalistic fervor of nations and churches. In secret prayer closets, He was preparing fervent young nationals such as Omar Cabrera for service in Argentina, Yonggi Cho in Korea, Washington Ngede in East Africa and P.J. Titus in India.

This did not leave out the Western missionary force either. Between 1969 and 1979, the number of Protestant missionaries from North America increased more than 50 percent.

When the massive new crop of independent, charismatic churches exploded on the American church scene in the early eighties, the institutions and agencies were already in place to service them. New recruits from these churches are now joining the international missionary team to become a force in the earth. Yes, the "funeral" of missions was extremely premature.

Significant Trends in Missions

The world-Christian movement is strong. As I have traveled around the world, I have come to two conclusions: 1) The world situation is worse than I had imagined, and 2) the church situation is better than I had imagined. The Holy Spirit is powerfully at work, often in places and through people we might least expect. We are gearing up for a massive ingathering of what may be the final harvest. In fact, C. Peter Wagner concludes, "We are in the springtime of Christian missions." [2]

The *internationalizing of missions* is, without question, the most important trend in missions today. If present rates continue, the Protestant missionary force from developing nations may project to over fifty thousand by the end of the century. [3] Some brothers and sisters from developing nations object to the use of the term *Third World* to describe their regions. They correctly observe that in many categories their regions are first or second. This thrilling new sense of ownership of the Great Commission by Christians from every nation is highly significant. Consider these exciting facts:

• During the twentieth century, Christianity has become the most extensive and universal religion in history.

• There are now more Christians in the Southern Hemisphere than in the Northern Hemisphere. The new centers of vitality for the church in many ways are Africa, Asia and Latin America. This more than counterbalances the decline in Western Europe.

• Each day welcomes a net global increase of at least seventy-eight thousand Christians.

• Each week approximately one thousand new

churches are planted in Asia and Africa alone.

• Christianity is now a genuinely international family of faith. Christianity has surged ahead in the world's less-developed countries—from 83 million believers in 1900 to 643 million by 1980.[4] From being predominantly white, Christianity is now an amalgam of the races and peoples of the world, with whites dropping from more than 80 percent to about 40 percent.

• The proportion of Christians to the whole population will increase in Asia more than in any other region of the world.

Christians in the Western world must open their eyes to this new reality: *The church of the historically Christian nations of the Northern Hemisphere is becoming the minority church in the world.*[5]

Another important trend in missions is the new surge of *local church involvement.* For years, even decades, missions conferences were out of style, particularly in charismatic churches. All that is changing. Many churches are even attempting to be their own mission agencies. There is a new understanding that the church is the legitimate, biblical "sender" of missionaries. As the Lausanne Covenant states, "The church is at the very center of God's cosmic purpose and is his appointed means of spreading the Gospel."

Unfortunately, charismatics still rank well below their traditional evangelical counterparts in missions giving. Of the top twenty U.S. churches in missions giving, not one of them is charismatic. This can and must change in the 1990s, not because we are in a competitive race with other evangelicals but because we must be better stewards of our resources.

Still, *charismatic involvement* is a massively significant trend in missions. The charismatic wing of the church is providing new pools of resources, both of people and finances, for missions. As stated earlier, we represent missions' awakening giant.

The *missiological expertise* that has emerged in the last two decades is a vital component for fulfilling the Great Commission. Resources only dreamed of a few years ago are now serviceable realities. The U.S. Center for World Mission in Pasadena is a beehive of innovative ideas for world evangelization. The contribution of David Barrett's *World Christian Encyclopedia* and the world evangelization data base of the Foreign Mission Board of the Southern Baptist Convention are libraries of information. Add to this the vast contributions of MARC (the Missions Advanced Research and Communication arm of World Vision International), the *Ethnolog* produced by Wycliffe Bible Translators and the ongoing research at the Fuller School of World Mission, and one sees that world evangelization has now become both a subjective passion and an objective science.

Short-term missionaries are also changing the landscape of missions. The term *missionary* was once reserved for those who viewed overseas service as their one and only career. But no longer. Roughly a third of all missionaries now serving are short-term. This slice of life dedicated to cross-cultural ministry usually colors the rest of one's life with a missions orientation.

Of course *power evangelism* will be a vital added

ingredient to much of missions in the nineties. Charismatics will always agree with the larger evangelical family that evangelism at its core is gospel proclamation with a view to the conversion of the hearer to Christ. However, in the next decade I look for addenda on this definition that include the credibility and desirability of power encounters to augment the message.

Since Ralph Winter's historic challenge at the 1974 Lausanne congress, the thrust of world missions has rightly focused more and more on the *hidden peoples*. Sometimes called unreached peoples, these masses of humanity represent the hidden half. Winter contends that the missions task should not necessarily be seen as preaching the gospel in geopolitical nations, but as planting a viable church within each ethnic group on earth. Winter estimates that some twelve thousand such groups still have little or no ongoing Christian witness. He maintains that this is in fact the great evangelistic task. This whole concept is exciting. Just thirty years ago we were "shooting in the dark," not really knowing where we stood in relation to the goal of world evangelization. Today we know precisely what remains to be done.

Tent-makers are of ever-growing importance to the future of world missions. A high percentage of nations already restricts conventional missionary activity. This percentage is expected to increase markedly by the year 2000. Yet productive, skilled Christians are warmly received in virtually every nation to work in areas of government, business and education. Just as Paul made tents to finance his missionary journeys, today's tent-makers receive their salaries from secular employers and live in a foreign land as witnesses for Jesus Christ.

Last, but certainly not least, *prayer networks* will act as an indispensable key to breaking down the demonic strongholds over nations. Prayer will pave the way for reception of the gospel. Historically, massive prayer always precedes revival. An encouraging trend is that more prayer is now being amassed worldwide than ever in history. This signals imminent global harvest.

Hearing God's Heartbeat

King David's mighty men were men of renown because, among other desirable qualities, they "had understanding of the times, to know what Israel ought to do" (1 Chr. 12:32). Daily I petition the Lord that I will not walk through these last years of the twentieth century half awake. I want every cell of my being to vibrate with life. Christians today need to stand not only against drugs but against the spirit that seeks to lull all of us into spiritual semiconsciousness.

When one looks at the unprecedented challenges facing us, it is natural to wonder where all the heroes are. Where are the missions enthusiasts of yesterday— those with the compassion of Amy Carmichael, the charisma of Bob Pierce or the stature of John R. Mott? Yet at a second glance I see that God sovereignly chose these people to serve Him in their generation; as amazing as it seems, He has chosen you and me to serve Him in our generation.

Costa Deir says, "Only those who see the invisible

can do the impossible.'' This ability to see with the eyes of faith sustained Moses during his preparatory wilderness years (see Heb. 11:27). It can also sustain us. Along with seeing the invisible, we must learn to hear the inaudible. Hearing God's voice—the inner witness of His Spirit—will be increasingly vital in the days ahead. Only those who cultivate the ability to hear God's voice in their spirits will discover the ever-unfolding strategy of the Holy Spirit for world evangelization. Our good ideas, even those nobly offered to God for His use and blessing, will not be sufficient to get the job done. Better, slicker ideas on evangelism are out there, now more than ever. Yet the world waits to be won. We must discover God's secrets for reaching the unreached. He will disclose His secrets only to those who have developed an intimacy with Him.

As we hear God's heartbeat, we discover again that His greatest priority is all the things that missions is about: the preeminence of His Son throughout the earth, destroying the works of the devil, establishing His kingdom and calling out a people for His name.

In the past, Pentecostals and charismatics have congratulated themselves for having ''picked up'' on different issues the Holy Spirit was spotlighting to the body of Christ. If we are to continue to ''pick up'' heaven's emphasis to the church, we must see what is currently shining in the bright light of the Spirit's display. There, illumined and center stage, we will see world evangelization.

Jack Hayford, pastor of Church on the Way in Van Nuys, California, wrote recently,

We are clearly at a watershed in the Church. There not only is a new millennium beckoning us to high faith and bold conquest, but a disturbing sense of the Holy Spirit now doing everything possible to get our attention to His desire. He wants to do the unprecedented through us, because the need around us is precisely that![6]

We should ask why the Holy Spirit has allowed different emphases over the past several years. Was there some overarching purpose, some grand whole into which all the other components fit? Why the emphasis on faith, prosperity or healing? Why was the Holy Spirit calling us to unity and prayer? Why was there a cry for a restoration of strong local churches or the establishing of the kingdom of God? Are not all of these important components of one integrating theme? None of these emphases, though important, is an end in itself. All are part of a grander scheme to produce a glorious church that will, in turn, reap the global harvest and bring glory to God. The Holy Spirit has issued these calls to prepare the church for the final thrust toward world evangelization.

God's call on the strong, younger charismatic churches is to flow with what the Holy Spirit is now saying. We cannot camp on an emphasis of a few years ago and assume it is the "now word" of the Spirit. The Holy Spirit is constantly active and dynamic. He is never static. If we park too long, even on an emphasis He has given, we may wake up to discover that the gentle Dove has moved on. As the countdown speeds toward 2000, we must catch the wave of the Spirit's directives, launching us into a world in need of Jesus as never before. Any church, charismatic or not, that does not emphasize missions in the nineties will be left out in the cold.

Reaping the Ripe Harvest

Bill Bright, founder of Campus Crusade for Christ, was asked what drives him to keep going for Christ. He replied, "The filling of the Holy Spirit and knowledge that the harvest is not forever. It soon will be past." On the clock of a beautiful church spire in Dallas two words are inscribed: Night cometh. In missions, there is always an underlying urgency. Masses are constantly slipping into a Christless eternity. Jesus said, "I must work the works of Him who sent Me while it is day; the night is coming when no one can work" (John 9:4). We cannot assume that today's outpouring of the Spirit is indefinite. We cannot presume that the fields will always be white.

On the farm, when it is time for harvest, everything else becomes secondary. It is not a time to clean the plows or strategize for the next year's harvest. The current harvest must capture everyone's time and energy. Before daylight and well into the night, the one agenda is safely bringing in the harvest. Our response to the harvest is a strong indicator of our effectiveness. "He who gathers in summer is a wise son; but he who sleeps in harvest is a son who causes shame" (Prov. 10:5).

When George Beverly Shea was growing up on the plains of Canada, his father took him to see the flowing wheat just before harvest. "Look, son," Shea's father observed, "the harvest is so big you can't see the fences." The harvest of souls worldwide is so big it dwarfs the fences of our disunity and all other obstacles.

Today's harvest is massive. But it will not reap itself. Laborers are needed. I repeat Jesus' challenge to us: "The harvest truly is plentiful, but the laborers are few. Therefore pray the Lord of the harvest to send out laborers into His harvest" (Matt. 9:37-38).

Where will we find these laborers? A vigorous potential army is all around us.

A Call to Youth

God calls people of every age to His service. But God always has His eye on the young generation.

God has always used young people. Perhaps it is because they don't know what the parameters are; if there's a big assignment to complete, they finish it first and ask questions later. Throughout the Bible when God had a big job to do He often called on a young person. And young people have always been at the forefront of the world missions march of the church. In the first era of missionary advance, God sent William Carey, not yet thirty, to defy the status quo and challenge the church to reach beyond its borders. In the second era it was again young men and women, including Hudson Taylor, David Livingstone and Mary Slessor, who made the difference. As the third era of missions dawned, young men, such as William Cameron Townsend and Donald McGavran, again changed the course of missions.

John R. Mott was instrumental in the early days of

the YMCA as well as the Student Volunteer Movement. When he was well over seventy, he made this observation to the YMCA staff: "We must be constantly weaving into our organization the new generation. My work the world over and across the many years has shown me that young people can be trusted with great loads and great responsibilities. Youth have never disappointed me when I have put heavy burdens on them." [7]

I frankly have confident faith that we are on the verge of a second, worldwide Jesus movement among young people. It may not carry the same names or take the same forms as the revival of the sixties and seventies. But it will, once again, be led by young people (some of whom are the sons and daughters of parents won to Christ in the first Jesus movement).

Committed for Conquest

I can see them as though it were yesterday. Singaporean youth crowded around me to ask all sorts of questions about American teenagers. "Do American youth appreciate their education as much as we do?" "Is it true that American teenagers go on dates without chaperones?" "Do they wear jeans all the time?"

These committed Asian young people had just told me of their desire to go into mainland China to share the gospel of Christ. Each of them told me they were willing to forego a career, to stay single and to die, if need be, to share Jesus with the Chinese.

"Tell me," the beautiful young woman inquired, "are American teenagers as committed to Jesus as we are?"

I swallowed hard and sputtered out a vague answer.

All around the world a new generation of young people is fully committed to Jesus and to world evangelism. They refuse to tolerate halfhearted commitment in themselves and cannot understand it in others. Yet the joy in their faces shows that their "sacrifices" aren't really that.

The 1980 Conference on World Evangelism in Pattaya, Thailand, issued a plea for two hundred thousand new missionaries by the year 2000. Where will they come from? Paul Borthwick gives the answer: "While many will go from the Third World into other parts of the world, there is still a great need for those to go from the West—including across cultural barriers here in the United States! Where will these servants come from? Our youth groups are excellent sources!"[8]

My heart aches when I see young people sign up for the Peace Corps or VISTA and overlook a missionary career. As fine as these organizations are, they do not touch the root need of the people they seek to help. I cry, O God, why haven't we told these kids that a career in missions will accomplish everything they could accomplish through a secular, humanitarian organization *plus* give people the answer to their greatest need—the good news of Jesus Christ!

Tony Campolo, a popular youth speaker and sociologist, understands the church's failure at this point:

> We in youth work have mistakenly assumed that the best way to relate to young people is to provide them with various forms of entertainment. For many of us there is no end to the building

of gymnasiums, the sponsoring of hayrides and the planning of parties. We would do better if we invited our young people to accept the challenge to heroically change the world.[9]

There is a growing number of Christian young people who are upchucking on selfishness. They want something more out of life, more out of themselves and more out of their Christianity.

One of my most earnest prayers for the young is that they will have a purpose in life that is big enough and worthy enough to demand every ounce of their ability, love and creativity. We in the church have been guilty of robbing youth of a world vision large enough to sink their teeth into for the rest of their lives. We should extend the same missionary challenge to today's youth that Francis Xavier, the great missionary to China and Japan, issued to the youth of his day. He urged students to "give up their small ambitions and come eastward to preach the gospel of Christ."

The torch is being passed on. Think of it! For almost two thousand years Christians have dreamed of finally fulfilling the Great Commission. And God has ordained that the young generation—this present generation—run the last lap. "But you are a chosen generation, a royal priesthood, a holy nation, His own special people, that you may proclaim the praises of Him who called you out of darkness into His marvelous light" (1 Pet. 2:9).

SEVEN

The Kingdom and the Rapture

It is not for you to know times or seasons which the Father has put in His own authority. But you shall receive power when the Holy Spirit has come upon you; and you shall be witnesses to Me in Jerusalem, and in all Judea and Samaria, and to the end of the earth.
—*Jesus Christ (Acts 1:7-8)*

A young boy always walked home from school past the big town clock. On one particular day, something went wrong with the reliable, old timepiece. It struck thirteen times. Terrified, the boy ran all the way home, threw open the door and shouted, "Mother, it's later than it's ever been before!"

No matter what one's eschatological position, there's no debate that it is later than it has ever been. A sense of urgency has always played a major role in missions motivation. Postmillennialists are driven to plant the kingdom. Premillennialists are driven to reach as many as possible before the Lord comes. All are driven to reach people before they die without Christ.

Discussions of eschatology, the study of the last times, are always potentially volatile, and friction over last-times theology has escalated sharply in recent years. (It seems to ebb and flow.) Because stiff disagreements over the end times threaten our missions effectiveness, the issue must be addressed. The "kingdom now" issue is potentially as divisive as the shepherding issue of a few years back.

Of course, I realize that one chapter in a book will not resolve the various differences. In fact, that is not my immediate concern. My goal is not even to defend my own position (which seems to be in constant flux). My concern is with the prospect of a dilution of strength and focus; we are often prone to turn our "guns" and energies on one another instead of marching as a unified army. Inevitably this hampers our missions potential.

Missionaries of the One-Way Ticket

Hal Lindsey's *The Late Great Planet Earth*, though written as something of a theological treatise, became one of the most effective evangelistic tools of all time. It also made dispensational premillennialism palatable to millions. Larry Norman sang a lament of those left behind after Christ's return: "I Wish We'd All Been Ready." The late sixties and early seventies saw a major reemphasis on prophecy and its tie to world events.

Thousands were brought to faith in Christ through an emphasis, not so much on the events of His first coming, but on the prospect of His second coming. Some may object to using the doctrine of the return of Christ as an evangelistic motivation. They argue that the second coming of Christ is the blessed hope of the believer; the nonbeliever needs to hear the message of His first coming to seek and save the lost.

Nevertheless, the call to prepare for a soon-coming, cataclysmic event has often pressed Christians into aggressive evangelism and non-Christians into the family of God. Not only was this the case with the Jesus movement; it has happened before in history, including at the turn of the century.

There were great eschatological hopes as the world entered the twentieth century. Missions enthusiasts spoke of "world evangelization in this generation," ensued by the coming of the Lord. Postmillennialists saw the first signs of what appeared to them to be "new heavens and a new earth in which righteousness dwells" (2 Pet. 3:13). There were only a few minor skirmishes around the globe. The spreading Christianization of the earth would surely bring an end to war itself. This euphoric optimism lasted even through World War I. This war was viewed by some postmillennialists as the final, necessary death groans of the old order before the inevitable new order of the kingdom of God was established. Americans, having paid a terrible price in the loss of men, were comforted in the hope that this was "the war to end all wars."

Some missionary hymns of the time picked up this battle cry to bring in the kingdom.

For the darkness shall turn to dawning,

A FORCE IN THE EARTH

And the dawning to noonday bright,
And Christ's great kingdom shall come on earth,
The kingdom of love and light.
                    —H. Ernest Nichol

In a poem which has become a cherished British hymn, "Jerusalem," author William Blake had urged Christians a hundred years earlier to continue to work for Christian social reform.

I will not cease from mental fight,
Nor shall my sword sleep in my hand
Till we have built Jerusalem
In England's green and pleasant land.

But in another later segment of Christendom, a Texas pastor was popularizing the teachings of J.N.N. Darby in a system of biblical interpretation known as dispensational premillennialism. C.I. Scofield first compiled his reference Bible as a teaching aid for missionaries. It soon became one of the most widely used tools for Bible study.

Early Pentecostals soundly rejected the conclusions of dispensational theology that prohibited certain gifts of the Spirit in this church age. According to Scofield's position, the need for spiritual gifts such as tongues, healing and miracles had ceased with the closing of the canon of Scripture. Pentecostals, having experienced outbreaks of all of the above, obviously could not accept this view. Nevertheless, most early Pentecostals did embrace Scofield's understanding of last things. They believed with Scofield that nothing stood in the way of Christ's catching away of His church. It could happen at any moment. It was the next great event on history's calendar.

This belief in the imminence of Christ's return was heightened for early Pentecostals by the outpouring of the Spirit in Topeka and Los Angeles. They were convinced that the renewing of biblical signs was a sure signal from heaven of Christ's soon return. Pentecostal missionaries fanned out across the globe almost immediately. They felt that everyone must be told of this fresh outpouring of the Spirit and warned to prepare for the Lord's return. The passion of their message convinced many hearers. This first wave of Pentecostal missionaries never expected to return from the field. They felt certain the Lord would come before they could come home. This early passion, accompanied with the anointing of the Holy Spirit, is at least part of the explanation for the amazingly rapid spread of the full-gospel message around the world. They were, as Vinson Synan says, "missionaries of the one-way ticket." One pioneer Pentecostal missionary put it this way: "It's just as close to heaven from India as it is from America."

The premillennial view sparked missionary activity for many. But other premillennialists chose another course.

Rock Till the Rapture or Take Charge?

While the belief in Christ's imminent return drove some to the ends of the earth, others were driven to a spiritual rocking chair. They became the theological equivalents of B.F. Skinner's psychological determinists. For them, everything was already determined.

Nothing could break the preordained pattern. A *que sera, sera* attitude froze the fire of many and plunged them into spiritual paralysis. They were rockin' till the rapture.

Naturally, there was a reaction. Christian activists reminded the disinterested that the Great Commission was still in force, no matter when Christ would return. Further, we had a cultural mandate as well as a Great Commission. At creation, God had said that humankind was to take dominion (see Gen. 1:26). It followed, according to this view, that redeemed humanity was to reclaim for God all that had been illegally taken by Satan. Therefore, Christians were to "take dominion" in every field of human activity including the arts, business, education and government. After all, they reasoned, Jesus had commanded us to occupy until He returns (see Luke 19:13). God's kingdom rule was to be enforced now. No more rocking till the rapture. God had ordained that we rule and reign "in this life."

The ineptness of much of the church in the sixties and seventies had given way to a vigorous local church movement in the eighties. Evangelicals and charismatics flexed their new spiritual muscles and determined that, as politics' "swing vote," they would no longer be ignored. Social evils would be addressed in dramatic fashion. Christians would not roll over and play dead while humanism spread through public education. The weakened church of a few years back was again becoming the church militant.

It was essentially a question of which (or who) comes first. Postmillennialists were driven to establish a kingdom so the King could come. Premillennialists were anxious to bring back the King so He could establish His kingdom. Both groups, then and now, were utterly sincere and committed.

Many Christians have been confused over these issues. Some have backed away, waiting for the dust to settle. Many believers warm to aspects of both positions—and chill to other aspects of both positions. Is it possible to live in the hope of Christ's return without espousing every aspect of dispensationalism? Is it possible to claim Christ's lordship over all of life without espousing every tenet of dominion theology?

Happily, the answer is *yes*.

Living in Dynamic Tension

Tension is not necessarily a bad word. It is possible— indeed, it is necessary in our day—to live in the reality of many healthy tensions. Much of the strength of our Christian faith is derived from apparent paradoxes. In fact, they are healthy tensions. For instance, there is the strong, healthy paradox of the sovereignty of God and the free will of humanity. Both doctrines are immutably true. Yet the strength of each is derived from the veracity of the other. One's theology is warped only when that person stresses one truth to the diminishing of the other.

One definition of tension is the stress of two balancing forces causing extension. One of the great needs of the church right now is the exertion of healthy tension pertaining to eschatology. Such a tension would then cause an extension of the gospel around the world.

The early church lived in this dynamic tension regarding Christ's return. They never heard the terms premillennial, postmillennial or amillennial. But they awakened each day with dual thrills in their hearts: 1) Jesus will probably come today, and 2) if He doesn't, the gospel will be further advanced by nightfall than it is now.

Evidently, through twenty centuries of systematizing our theology, we have polarized these hopes. But why should we? The early church lived in the healthy tension of planting the kingdom while waiting for the rapture. We can too.

In this case, one's practical theology is more important than his or her systematic theology. The vital issue is not so much what a person believes about the end times. The greater issue is this: What is that person doing in light of those personal beliefs?

We often emphasize the points of eschatology that divide us. Here it is important to remember those commonly held beliefs that bind us, no matter what our millennial position. In the January 1988 issue of the *Evangelical Missions Quarterly*, there was an excellent, cordial discussion among Bible scholars of the millennium and missions. At the end of the conversation, David Hesselgrave concluded, "It should be clear that all of these theologians believe in the same gospel; that the first priority of the church is to take the gospel to all men everywhere; that man's eternal destiny is involved; and that the missionary task is an urgent one."[1]

All of Scripture can and should be viewed in this

healthy tension of planting the kingdom while waiting for the rapture. Jesus reminded us of the urgency of our task when He said that "the night is coming when no one can work" (John 9:4). Paul, who was also driven by urgency, said, "The night is far spent, the day is at hand" (Rom. 13:12). Is this a contradiction? Far from it! It is a classic case of healthy tension. "Night is coming"; therefore, we are urgent. "Light is coming"; therefore, we are optimistic.

The same dynamic tension can be seen regarding the present control of this planet. Postmillennialists work from the premise, "The earth is the Lord's, and all its fullness, the world and those who dwell therein" (Ps. 24:1). Premillennialists caution that "the whole world lies under the sway of the wicked one" (1 John 5:19). Who is right? The Bible is right! Again this is not a contradiction. Rather it is an antinomy.

An antinomy occurs where two equally valid principles run on two parallel tracks. To our eyes they apparently never meet. But somewhere out there, beyond our ability to see, there is a point of intersection. Each millennial position contains elements of truth. These truths, though seemingly running on parallel tracks, intersect in the infinite mind of God. We only grasp bits and pieces.

This is why unnecessary dogmatism regarding the end times is so dangerous. The growing Christian readily confesses that he or she does not have all the answers. She is still a learner. He still sits at the feet of Jesus for further revelation on this and every subject.

Let us hear and heed the cautions coming from our

brothers and sisters in both camps. The "Jesus is coming" camp warns those in the "kingdom now" camp not to let the kingdom of God degenerate into earthly agendas. Jesus clearly said, "My kingdom is not of this world" (John 18:36). Further, it is always tragic to diminish the second coming of Christ; it is the believer's blessed hope.

Conversely, the "kingdom now" camp warns the "Jesus is coming" camp not to capitulate to the spirit of the age. God "always leads us in triumph in Christ" (2 Cor. 2:14). Christ calls His church to a militant posture against Satan.

Those with a "Jesus is coming" orientation to missions believe that, by fulfilling the Great Commission, they take part in "hastening the coming of the day of God" (2 Pet. 3:12). We can have a part in bringing back the King! Since He is coming soon, there is absolutely no time to waste.

Those with a "kingdom now" orientation to missions observe that Christ's commission was not to steal a remnant but to take nations. A glorious church is at the center of God's evangelistic arsenal. World evangelization cannot be separated theologically from the kingdom of God. The gospel inevitably transforms culture.

Every statement in the last four paragraphs I espouse in healthy tension. I am engaged in aggressively planting the kingdom while eagerly awaiting the rapture.

Why Hasn't Jesus Returned?

No matter what your view on the second coming, one fact is obvious: It hasn't happened yet. Some very sincere Christians thought it would happen before this book reaches the press. First they predicted September 1988, giving eighty-eight reasons why Christ would certainly return then. When He didn't show up, the spokesman from Arkansas revised his forecast to September 1989.

I have no problem with urging people to be ready for Jesus' return. But I have a major disagreement with the gentleman from Arkansas who gave us his eighty-eight reasons for a specific date. And I am grieved over the responses of some Christians to his prediction. The responses often ranged from ridiculous to tragic. I'm still trying to figure out why some Christians were afraid of the prospect of Christ's return! The believer who is right with the Lord *longs* to see Him.

Why, I keep asking, was there so much talk about the return of Jesus with so little talk of fulfilling the Great Commission? They go hand in hand.

When we probe why Jesus has not yet returned, several reasons clearly emerge. For one thing, Jesus has not yet returned because of *an unprepared bride*. When Christ is exalted over all, the shout will go up, "Let us be glad and rejoice and give Him glory, for the marriage of the Lamb has come, and His wife has made herself ready" (Rev. 19:7). At present, vast portions of the redeemed remain unprepared for His coming. It is possible, as a Christian, to blush at the return of the Lord because you are unprepared. "And now, little children, abide in Him, that when He appears, we may have confidence and not be ashamed before Him at His coming" (1 John 2:28). Jesus gave His church one clear command to fulfill before He returned. Certainly, if that one command goes unfulfilled, it will be cause for being "ashamed before Him."

Further, Jesus has not returned because there is yet *an unrestored church*. In the last several years, many churches have experienced a measure of the restoration of New Testament power and anointing. But there is so much more to come! The church's greatest days are still ahead.

Fifty years ago, George Truett, long-time pastor of the First Baptist Church of Dallas, predicted, "The greatest churches in the world haven't been built yet." I believe that prediction is a prophecy—one that still holds true.

God has gone to great lengths in the past few years to exercise His purifying love for His church. What may have been temporary setbacks will work for the ultimate good of the church and her restoration.

This emphasizes another reason why Jesus has not yet returned: *an undying love* He has for all humanity.

> The Lord is not slow in keeping His promise, as some understand slowness. He is patient with you, not wanting anyone to perish, but everyone to come to repentance.
>
> But the day of the Lord will come like a thief. The heavens will disappear with a roar; the elements will be destroyed by fire, and the earth and everything in it will be laid bare.
>
> Since everything will be destroyed in this way, what kind of people ought you to be? You ought to live holy and godly lives as you look forward

to the day of God and speed its coming (2 Pet. 3:9-12, NIV).

Christ's undying love for humanity constrains Him from coming in judgment until the last possible second, waiting for the complete harvest of humanity to be gathered in. God has compassionately linked the time-table of Jesus' return to His concern for the perishing.

Remarkably, Peter says we can be instruments of God in speeding the coming of the day of God. This brings us to yet another reason why Jesus has not returned: *an unfinished task.* Untold millions are still untold. Christ's Great Commission to His church has not been rescinded. The task is yet unfinished, though remarkable strides are being made. Richard Lovelace, professor of church history at Gordon-Conwell Theological Seminary, speaks pointedly to the unfinished task.

> Let us remember that Jesus Christ is not to return again physically until the gospel has first been preached to all nations....I am not insisting that every nation must experience the degree of cultural infusion which Christianity has attained in the West. But it seems that the millions of Muslims and Chinese should gain something more than a brief glimpse of a flare shot off over another country.[2]

When will Christ return? I do not know. Nor do you. Nor do the scholars who have written on the subject. There are, however, two things I am sure of: 1) I am to live in the healthy tension of planting the kingdom while waiting for the rapture, and 2) the return of Jesus

Christ is somehow tied to closure of the Great Commission. "And this gospel of the kingdom will be preached in all the world as a witness to all the nations, and then the end will come" (Matt. 24:14).

Bringing the gospel to all people groups will require a laser focus on world evangelization. A strong commitment to the job can intensify our focus. But it also will require supernatural power. We cannot generate that quality, no matter how deeply committed we are. The Holy Spirit alone produces supernatural power and anointing. That part in world evangelization is uniquely His. It is for that purpose He has been given.

As always, Jesus refocuses His disciples on priority number one. Having been asked an eschatological question of when the kingdom would be restored, He basically said, "Gentlemen, it's none of your business. What *is* your business is getting the gospel to the ends of the earth."

"It is not for you to know the times or dates the Father has set by his own authority. But you will receive power when the Holy Spirit comes on you; and you will be my witnesses in Jerusalem, and in all Judea and Samaria, and to the ends of the earth" (Acts 1:7-8, NIV).

EIGHT

The Why of the Prosperity Message

Why should anyone hear the gospel twice until everyone has heard it once?—Oswald J. Smith

The first sermon I preached was in the spring of 1966. I was sixteen. In retrospect, I find it interesting that my text was 1 John 2:2: "And He Himself is the propitiation for our sins, and not for ours only but also for the whole world." This text foreshadowed the course my life and entrusted ministry would take. "He is the propitiation for our sins"—that's evangelism. "Not for ours only but also for the whole world"—that's missions. Evangelism and missions have continued to be my heartbeat.

So it is sometimes difficult for me to understand why all Christians do not share a passion for world evangelization—as soon as possible. To me, it seems one of the clearest, most integrating themes of our faith. When one makes a commitment to world missions as a high priority, one's values undoubtedly will change. That person will experience a shift in thinking and in the distribution of time and personal resources. The same holds true for churches. When a church gives missions more than tacit endorsement, there will be a redistribution of its resources. Where our money goes is always an excellent indicator of where our hearts really are.

Right Premise, Wrong Conclusions

Some years ago a new emphasis was heralded by many charismatic Bible teachers. Some disdainfully called it "the health and wealth gospel." Others termed it "the prosperity message." By whatever name, this emphasis spotlighted the effect of the gospel on personal and ministry finances.

No matter how noble the motives of some of its teachers, few would question that the emphasis on material prosperity has sometimes been abused and even perverted. Unfortunately, some have tried to baptize blatant materialism with biblical proof texting. This is quite simply a transgressing of the spirit of the Scriptures and the life-style of Jesus Himself. God's Word majestically refuses to be the cheerleader of any man-made political or economic system. It stands as the objective judge on all subjects, including economics.

Sometimes people gravitated toward the prosperity message because they saw in it a way to endorse their financial gluttony scripturally. Since God is a God of abundance and we are His children, they reasoned that we should have all things in abundance. This message appealed to the inherent greed in people. Yet greed and the tendency to hoard are categorically denounced throughout Scripture.

Here again is a tragic picture of how a wrong conclusion was deduced from a correct premise. God *is* a God of abundance. Indeed, He *does* desire to shower His children with all kinds of blessings. But we are wrong to conclude that these blessings are to stay exclusively ours. With Abraham, and as his spiritual seed, we are blessed for the expressed purpose of blessing others.

Why Prosperity?

What was the Holy Spirit telling us? Was He trying to turn us into insensitive financial tycoons who, from time to time, would give to God in a patronizing manner? Certainly not. Rather He was providing us a chance at financial freedom for missions expansion.

I am convinced that the Holy Spirit emphasized prosperity in the 1980s to equip economically the church for global harvest in the 1990s. If we are not merely playing word games, we must face the reality that it will take billions of dollars to fulfill the Great Commission. However unspiritual it may seem, in this fallen world, there are some things only money can do. No one has yet discovered a printing press in heaven that will, through faith alone, print and distribute Bibles world-wide. We have not yet found a way to satisfy the financial obligations of those who construct churches, hospitals and schools with anything other than money. All missionaries, including "faith missionaries," will tell you that, at some point, faith must be translated into cash. Evangelistic endeavors take money. Missions advances take money. And even in ministries to the poor, somebody has to buy the soup.

The Holy Spirit emphasized financial prosperity to liberate us from debt and from a poverty mentality. God knew that if we were to seize the immense, seasonal opportunities of this pivotal decade, we would need mega-thinkers who were not afraid to invest multi-millions in missions. So He hammered away at the poverty mentality that had historically choked our endeavors. And He raised our level of faith so we could believe Him for increase in our finances.

We may have made a terrible miscalculation, however. Instead of using our new financial strength to liberate us from existing financial strain, we sometimes used it as a line of credit for even greater indebtedness. For whatever reasons, many ministries appeared to try to validate their worth by building bigger and better. Of course God wants us to succeed in ministry. Any structure built to the glory of God should be worthy of Him and be a fitting expression of His character. But a "success syndrome," a drive to keep up with the appearances of success whether we're succeeding or not, has infested much of the church. On this tenuous theology-philosophy that success is measured primarily by what we can see or touch, we have mortgaged our hopes well into the next century and weighed down our present opportunities with an albatross of debt.

What then constitutes true prosperity or true success? To escape the ghetto and get a college education is success for the young person who is born in that ghetto. But it was also success for C.T. Studd to give his fortune to missions and become a faith missionary. It was success for Jim Elliot to say no to a career in America, bury himself in the obscure, Ecuadorian jungle and face eventual martyrdom. We cannot afford to view success through the world's distorted lenses. Plainly and simply, success is to know God's will for your life and do it joyfully.

The question then is not whether or not one has wealth. Rather the question is how that wealth is being utilized. As Jerry Cook observed, "What I am doing with my resources says infinitely more about my spiritual condition than does the fact that I have them." [1]

The Need for Balance

As with so many biblical issues, the whole prosperity issue calls for a balanced response. Millions can affirm the truth of Jesus' claim that life does not consist in the abundance of things a person possesses. I've driven through Beverly Hills. I've also been in the crowded, garbage-heaped slums of Mexico City. I discovered one commonality in both environments: desperate people.

Without question poverty is an insult to the dignity of persons. But the proclivity toward sophisticated idolatry among the rich is equally dehumanizing. Jesus has set a clear example for His followers and certainly for His ambassadors. We are to identify with the poor, the weak, the dispossessed. According to Jesus, the priority of gospel proclamation is first to the poor. We cannot close our ears to the cries of the physically hungry in the ghetto or the spiritually hungry in the mansions. It is the same gospel—with the same demands —for a poor leper or a rich, young ruler.

To come to grips with the implications of the gospel is to come to grips with sacrifice. At times in the last few years I have blushed with shame at how some charismatics have heralded a message almost directly counter to the teachings of Jesus. Some have even inferred that sacrifice is either unspiritual or unscriptural. Whose Bible are they reading?

Heroic stories, of laying aside fortunes for missionary work, of investing one's life in a remote jungle habitation, sound almost senseless to many today. What's the point? some seem to ask with a chuckle. Some have stressed that "Jesus died to give us the good life"— and then left the message there. They've inferred that the "good life" was based on material wealth. While Christians in the past measured their success by the strength of their piety, we often seem to measure our success by the strength of our pocketbooks. God's Word reminds us not to equate spirituality with financial blessings. Gain is not necessarily godliness.

In fact, we are to disassociate from those who equate the two. Faith is never to be used for carnal ends. Paul describes those who attempt to use faith in this fashion:

They suppose that godliness is a means of gain.

From such withdraw yourself.

But godliness with contentment is great gain.

For we brought nothing into this world, and it is certain we can carry nothing out.

And having food and clothing, with these we shall be content.

But those who desire to be rich fall into temptation and a snare, and into many foolish and harmful lusts which drown men in destruction and perdition.

For the love of money is a root of all kinds of evil, for which some have strayed from the faith in their greediness, and pierced themselves through with many sorrows.

But you, O man of God, flee these things and pursue righteousness, godliness, faith, love, patience, gentleness (1 Tim. 6:5-11).

An Abundance for Every Good Work

I stress again that I am not against material prosperity itself. Nor is the Bible. The Bible is not against having riches. It is against hoarding riches. As a Christian, it is not inordinate for you to expect a dependable car, a comfortable home and financial security for your family. It is, however, not only inordinate but immoral to develop a ravenous lust for ''more'' because you have been convinced that life does indeed consist in the abundance of things that a person possesses. This is in polar antithesis to the teaching of Jesus. Jesus said,

Do not lay up for yourselves treasures on earth,

> where moth and rust destroy and where thieves break in and steal; but lay up for yourselves treasures in heaven, where neither moth nor rust destroys and where thieves do not break in and steal.
>
> For where your treasure is, there your heart will be also (Matt. 6:19-21).

While poverty itself is not God's will, Christians may choose voluntarily to lower their standard of living to improve their standard of life. Such sacrificial acts are in keeping with the servant motif of genuine Christian living. They remind us that the true riches Jesus spoke of are not material.

Involuntary lack, on the other hand, has its origin with the one whose purpose is to steal, kill and destroy. In contrast, Jesus Christ has come to give abundant life on every level. And having the capacity to give generously is a joyous experience. God desires that we understand the rhythm of sowing, reaping and then sowing again in greater measure. It is a principle He has weaved into the fabric of the universe.

> But this I say: He who sows sparingly will also reap sparingly, and he who sows bountifully will also reap bountifully.
>
> So let each one give as he purposes in his heart, not grudgingly or of necessity; for God loves a cheerful giver.
>
> And God is able to make all grace abound toward you, that you, always having all sufficiency in all things, have an abundance for

every good work (2 Cor. 9:6-8).

Certainly world missions is a "good work." God desires that we have an abundance to "sow" into missions. Spiritually or financially, you cannot impart what you do not possess.

Recently I was invited to lecture at a leading evangelical seminary on the distinctives of Pentecostal/ charismatic missiology. In the question and answer session that followed, one student objected to what he felt was the mishandling by some charismatic teachers of 3 John 2. That verse says, "Beloved, I pray that you may prosper in all things and be in health, just as your soul prospers."

I agreed with the student that it is correct exegetically to understand that this is an apostolic greeting from John to Gaius. But I suggested that it is incorrect to deduce that the intent cannot be broadened. For one thing, simple, trusting believers have taken this prayer as a personal promise through the centuries, and they have grown in faith because of it. I reminded this seminary student that God is far more prone to bless simple faith than He is enlightened exegesis. Further, if John prayed for this as a good thing for one of God's children, should we not also desire prosperity and health for all His children? And if we take the hermeneutical liberty of personalizing other verses, such as prayers by the apostle Paul for the different churches, can we not by the same standard personalize this apostolic benediction?

As I supported this position, a furloughing missionary of that denomination came to my aid. He reminded all of us that it was quite convenient as upper-middle-class, armchair theologians to debate prosperity. He suggested that those best qualified to weigh the merits of prosperity are those who consistently feel the pangs of hunger and oppression.

The Bible cautions all Christians against greed and trusting in uncertain riches. I have noticed that greed has nothing to do with income or wealth. There is a proclivity toward greed among both rich and poor. As Christians, we cannot embrace this spirit of mammon, whether we live in affluence or need. But for those who are blessed financially, the warning is doubly strong. Paul told the young pastor Timothy to remind his wealthy parishioners to invest in lasting riches.

> Command those who are rich in this present age not to be haughty, nor to trust in uncertain riches but in the living God, who gives us richly all things to enjoy.
>
> Let them do good, that they be rich in good works, ready to give, willing to share, storing up for themselves a good foundation for the time to come, that they may lay hold on eternal life (1 Tim. 6:17-19).

Perceptive Christians realize that, in reality, they do not possess wealth—they steward it. All blessings come from God and ultimately belong to Him. The Bible says we are to be "good stewards of the manifold grace of God" (1 Pet. 4:10). Good financial stewardship is summed up well in the sage counsel of John Wesley: "Gain all you can, save all you can, give all you can."

Identifying With the Global Church

If Christians in the Western world are to identify with their brothers and sisters worldwide, both sides will have to reassess the issue of money. The church in the West must vastly augment its gifts of love to the world's needy. We must commit ourselves especially to our brothers and sisters in developing nations. Scripture clearly commands us to feed the hungry, clothe the naked and give hope to the disenfranchised. In country after country I have watched pastors tearfully request literature. In our nation Christian books are marketed with finesse. But in many nations, vast numbers of literate Christians long for a Bible. Pastors who do have a copy of God's Word often do not have basic tools, such as a concordance and Bible dictionary, to help them in ministry. Christian books are often scarce or even nonexistent.

We cannot turn away from the screaming needs of the world. Even the most casual observer concludes that wealth and poverty are juxtaposed within the nations. Around the world the rich nations are getting richer and the poor are getting poorer. Any comprehensive strategy of evangelization must address the worldwide epidemics of disease, hunger and illiteracy. As charismatic Christians, we believe Jesus is acutely concerned with humanity's needs on every level. Our Savior is also the great Physician. The gospel we offer is a whole gospel for a fractured world. While we may differ on the nuances of God's kingdom rule, we all agree His lordship over the nations starts now. The gospel we espouse heralds salvation in a sinful world, healing in a broken world, peace in a war-torn world, justice in an oppressed world and hope in a pessimistic world.

In the days ahead the primary missions role of Christians in the West may well be to finance the powerful, indigenous churches and missionary enterprises now emerging throughout developing nations. And as we give to those in need, we must guard against any judgmentalism or paternalism. We must give simply because the love of God compels us.

Yes, the church in the West must change its attitude toward money. We must gladly "sow" into the church worldwide. When we pour money for gospel advance into needy regions, we should fully expect the gospel to do in those areas what it has done for Western Europe and the United States. Just look at history. Wherever the gospel has dominated, there has inevitably been attendant upward mobility. The fallout of the gospel in any nation is always good. People are lifted and thus the nation is lifted.

Poverty is a blight. It is demeaning and dehumanizing to have insufficient money to pay one's bills, to respond to the heart's promptings to give, to invest for the future.

I've seen firsthand the plight of the world's poor and dispossessed. Everything I know about God and His character convinces me that it is inconceivable that God could be honored by the degrading effects of poverty on the human spirit. It is also clear to any who give history even a slight overview that the gospel has an inherent lift in it. The gospel lifts the crushing loads of guilt, despair and, yes, poverty. Some sociologists have postulated very plausible theories of the tie between the Protestant Reformation and the Industrial Revolution, the first being the cause and the latter being the effect. Others speak of a "Protestant work ethic," stating that a life based on glorifying God lifted Europe out of both the economic and spiritual doldrums of the Middle Ages. Undoubtedly these factors were present. God delights in propelling people to their full potential.

So while we in the West must repent of any paternalism in our giving, those in developing nations must receive with dignity and themselves begin to give. *Only* by giving, even out of their acute need, will they escape the clutches of generational poverty. They must radically turn from a receiving life-style to a giving life-style. One of the first precepts I teach church leadership in developing nations is this: "Find a way, every day, to give something to God and something to people." This is the path to true freedom. There must be a renouncing of pretentious materialism on the one hand and of a poverty mentality on the other hand.

It is God's desire for His church in every nation to prosper. Then the needy will see that our God generously cares for His children; they will see that He is a God of mercy and blessing. In a world where hundreds of millions will go to bed hungry tonight, that is good news.

Cars or Countries?

Faith does indeed get results. Frankly, you probably can confess your way into a forty-thousand-dollar car (with considerable help from our free-enterprise system). While it is certainly no sin to drive a nice car, the relative

131

value of such faith confessions should be brought up for review. At the judgment seat of Christ more than one faith-confessing charismatic will have to sputter out a reason why he chose to claim classy cars instead of countries.

One man defended himself by saying, "I never had nice things like this when I was young. Now I'm getting to have them." Again, there is nothing wrong with nice things. God created some things purely for the purposes of aesthetics and joy. Nevertheless, if you think the Lord is giving you these blessings to convince you somehow of your value and worth, you are still tying meaning to possessions. That is a warped, even sick, view of things. More than a new car, you need a new touch from Jesus, a touch to heal you of a poor self-image tenuously tied to possessions. According to the Lord of all wealth, life does *not* consist in the abundance of things a person possesses.

Charismatics pride themselves in their heritage from early Pentecostal pioneers. But if we see ourselves as their true spiritual offspring, we must respect their values. Horace McCracken recounts that, in the early years of the Pentecostal outpouring, "whole families volunteered for the world, sold their possessions, and started for the field. They were possessed with a passion to go to the ends of the earth for their Lord, and no sacrifice seemed too great for them that the Gospel might be proclaimed and the coming of the Lord might be hastened."[2] That is how the Pentecostal message spread so rapidly around the world. Those early Pentecostal missionaries lived and died agreeing with missionary-great C.T. Studd, "If Jesus Christ be God and died for me, then no sacrifice is too great for me to give for Him."

Let us be careful where we target our faith, for it will surely be honored. God promises, "Ask of Me, and I will give You the nations for Your inheritance, and the ends of the earth for Your possession" (Ps. 2:8).

In Christ's new order the most vulnerable are not the risk takers but the self-protective. "For whoever desires to save his life will lose it, but whoever loses his life for My sake and the gospel's will save it" (Mark 8:35). The exciting irony of the Christian adventure is that under the new covenant we give to receive, we profit by losing, and we find our lives by laying them down. The follower of Jesus is first a producer, not a consumer. The follower's emphasis is serving, not being served. The disciple remembers the words of our Lord, "It is more blessed to give than to receive" (Acts 20:35).

World missionary advance is the why—and the redeeming social value—of the prosperity message.

NINE

Toward the Twenty-first Century

*The most important current trend is the inter-
nationalization of the church and the accompanying shift in the church's center of gravity.
The church's dynamic center is moving from
North Atlantic nations to the newer, more vital
churches of Latin America, Africa and Asia.*
—Howard Snyder

Over a decade ago the late David Watson, a godly leader of the charismatic renewal in Britain, predicted there would be three major forces at the close of the century: communism, Islam and Third-World Christianity. He suggested that Christianity in the West would probably be too self-indulgent to be a global factor.[1]

What kind of world are we facing as we move toward the twenty-first century? Let's take a look.

The Real War

In many ways Watson's prediction was prophetic, though with some encouraging twists. Communism, as an ideology, is worn out. On every continent it has proven to be ineffective; however, it is still a formidable force because of its massive military arsenals. The ailing, aging Bear of Bolshevism is still unpredictable. But few would now espouse communism as "the wave of the future." Such notions are incredulous almost to the point of amusement.

It would be interesting to know the story of the seeds of the 1989 democratic student uprisings in China. No doubt the parents of some of those students were devotees of the radical Red Guard, the vicious movement some twenty years ago that sought to purge China of non-Maoist elements including Christianity. How interesting that the innate longings for liberty could not be extracted from the hearts of their own children. If the full story were told, I suspect we would hear that the widespread acceptance of the gospel played a major role in the hopes of the brave Chinese students in Tiananmen Square for the democratization of their country.

Polish voters have roundly rejected communism. The martyrs in Hungary's democratic uprising of 1956 are now publicly lauded as the heroes they are. And communist Albania, which has brutally attempted to crush all religion, must concede massive failure. New reports leaked out of Albania suggest that Christians comprise up to 30 percent of the population.

While communism may be dying, Islam is very much alive. The whole world is aware of the terrorist tactics of some Islamic groups. The spread of Islam in the last few years has been rapid, often at the point of a sword or the end of a gun barrel. Yet we cannot deny its grip on some 20 percent of the earth's population. No serious prayer or discussion regarding world evangelism can avoid the Muslim world. In the nineties, Islam will replace communism as the great competitor with Christianity for the generation's hearts and minds. And the harsh fact is that Christianity will not penetrate the Muslim world on a major scale without a significant number of martyrs.

Still all is not well in Islam. The ever-changing world supply and demand for oil has pointed some once-wealthy nations in the Arab oil cartel toward fiscal distress. Millions of Muslims are embarrassed by Islam's more belligerent exponents. This has produced widespread discontent as more and more Muslims search for a true knowledge of God and His ways. While it cannot be said that Muslims are yet turning to Christ in massive numbers, it is true that more seeking Muslims are coming to Christ than ever before.

As I said previously, it seems clear that most religions are becoming more militant. Christianity as well is becoming more militant but with an important difference. Our aggression is motivated by love, not hate. And our arsenal is not material, but spiritual.

> For though we walk in the flesh, we do not war according to the flesh.
> For the weapons of our warfare are not carnal but mighty in God for pulling down strongholds, casting down arguments and every high

thing that exalts itself against the knowledge of God, bringing every thought into captivity to the obedience of Christ (2 Cor. 10:3-5).

As religions are perceived as increasingly militant, many will turn to the New Age movement as "the peaceful alternative." The rationale will be that religions engender strife and divisions among people. Instead of espousing war-prone religion, New Agers will "evangelistically" urge peace lovers to "tune in to yourself and the harmony in the universe." Christianity must counter this false yet formidable message by regaining the peace initiative. We must clearly and lovingly proclaim that peace—personal, national and international—can come only when the Prince of Peace rules.

In the past, Western Christianity has indeed been self-indulgent. The charismatic wing of Christendom has by no means escaped. But things are changing. We are once again focusing on ultimate issues. The give-me-what-I-want-now immaturity is surrendering to the exclamation of a full-grown church: "Give Him exaltation over all the earth." As Watson predicted, the church in developing nations is exceedingly strong. The church in the West now realizes that it is, in some ways, a junior partner with vigorous, younger churches worldwide. Together we are engaged in the real war—the cosmic, spiritual warfare for the allegiance of the human race. The global body of Christ is marching toward global conquest!

Charismatic Vitality

Enter the charismatic movement. God has engineered this global, spiritual renewal to be an energizer for missions. Into the total world missionary movement, charismatics and Pentecostals bring certain distinctives in deployment, strategy and theology. While these factors may not be unique to us, they are always clearly present.

Charismatics are sensitive to the Holy Spirit's directives in the deploying of missionaries. They believe that *the final word on the when and where of going belongs not to boards or agencies but to the Holy Spirit*. This is in keeping with the commissioning of missionaries by the first-century church at Antioch. "As they ministered to the Lord and fasted, the Holy Spirit said, 'Now separate to Me Barnabas and Saul for the work to which I have called them.' Then, having fasted and prayed, and laid hands on them, they sent them away" (Acts 13:2-3).

Listening for the Spirit's guidance has prompted Pentecostals and charismatics sometimes to defy conventional methods and commission large numbers of youth, single women and men, and lay persons as missionaries. Now many noncharismatic agencies are reassessing their deployment policies and utilizing these vast human resources as well.

Today's missions strategies among charismatics are yielding some of the most dramatic church growth worldwide. One particularly important aspect of global charismatic growth is the belief in *apostolic figures over a network of churches*. While many evangelicals continue to debate the legitimacy of apostles and prophets today, charismatics unashamedly refer to a "fivefold ministry." These five office gifts to the church are stated in Ephesians 4:11, "And He Himself gave some to be apostles, some prophets, some evangelists, and some pastors and teachers."

Once at an evangelical college I was challenged by a professor to show from Scripture that the gifts of apostles and prophets were still functioning. The professor seemed somewhat embarrassed to be reminded that the answer was right in the context of the Ephesians 4 passage. Paul specifically states these gifts to be in effect "till we all come to the unity of the faith" (v. 13). I respectfully suggested that his very invitation to debate was evidence that we had not yet reached a unity of the faith!

Charismatics argue that the apostolic gift is, in fact, the missionary gift, particularly as it relates to the planting of new works. In the United States, there are networks of churches relating to an apostolic figure who serves as a pastor to other pastors within that movement. But the most dramatic examples are overseas. Hundreds of pastors relate to Benson Idahosa in Nigeria. Ezekiel Guti has spawned hundreds of churches in Zimbabwe, as has Washington Ngede in Kenya, Tanzania and Uganda, and P.J. Titus in India. The most high-profile exhibit of apostolic authority is still Paul Yonggi Cho, pastor of the largest church in the history of Christendom. Not only has Cho's Yoido Full Gospel Church in Seoul birthed many other churches throughout South Korea; they have started churches in several other nations. And thousands of pastors of all denominations and many nations sit at the feet of this humble servant to learn principles of church growth.

While apostolic figures have decidedly advanced the gospel, these apostles themselves now hold the key to the next step toward evangelization of their nations. Since most of these men (and in a few cases women) are very strong personalities, they tend to be independent and wary of cooperation. This must be overcome. The next logical step toward total evangelization is for these networks to form a grid that will blanket those nations with the gospel. This is one of my specific, daily prayers.

Another distinctive of charismatic and Pentecostal strategy is *the centrality of the church*. Most often, local churches are constructed before schools, orphanages or hospitals. This strong local church orientation sees Christian community and ministry flowing from the church and back into it. Indigenous, charismatic-oriented churches are sprouting all over the world. As Jack Hayford says, we must develop "world class churches" intent on reaching the world.

Since the early days of the Pentecostal revival, *literature* has played an important part in promoting the message. Once again, charismatics and Pentecostals are at the forefront of the production and distribution of gospel literature. An exciting development is that more and more publishing is being done in the countries of distribution. Many thrilling stories are leaking out of how Bibles and gospel publications are being printed and distributed right under the noses of unsuspecting, anti-Christian authorities. Since the Reformation, literature has been at the forefront of the expansion of Christianity.

A vital point of Pentecostal-charismatic missions strategy is the high priority that has always been given to *urban ministry*. Pentecostals have been racially integrated from the beginning. Blacks, Hispanics and other minorities have always been a major force in American Pentecostalism. In America and around the world, the major evangelical presence in the major inner cities is often charismatic or Pentecostal churches. While many denominations have fled to suburbia, Pentecostals and charismatics have remained to offer hope to crowded urban dwellers.

Charismatic Theology and Missions

Charismatic theology lends itself to world missions in several important ways. First, charismatics guard *a high view of Scripture*. The vast majority of charismatics and Pentecostals believe in the full inerrancy of Scripture. Some denominations who until recently have been known for their leadership in missions are now wading through battles over biblical authority. While neo-orthodoxy has made some minor encroachments, most charismatics believe the Bible to be God's ultimate "thus saith the Lord." Further, charismatics are quick to act on biblical promises while some traditional evangelicals hesitate in exegetical discussions. This mentality ("If the Bible says it, let's do it") is vital to the effectiveness of missions.

Second, charismatics unashamedly endorse *an*

experiential Christianity. Their faith is more than a creed. Charismatics are not first cerebral about Christianity; they *feel* it. Some evangelicals decry this as a subjective orientation. Charismatics agree that the great planks of Christianity are grounded in objective truth. However, they do not believe this divorces faith from experience. Charismatic Christianity is objective truth that is subjectively experienced.

Nonexperiential forms of Christianity are, in fact, subbiblical. Often they have their roots in secular forms of unscriptural rationalism. And for most of the world, the first contact with religion is not through the mind but through the emotions. Animists will never be won to Christ through apologetics. Muslims must not only *hear* the unique message of the gospel; they must *see* and *feel* it if they are to respond positively. Most of the world has a supernatural orientation. The only Christianity that will be embraced on a global scale will be supernatural Christianity. Christianity is far more than the best of competing philosophies; it is an ever-growing love relationship between God and people through His mediating Son, Jesus Christ. It is this personal Jesus who, in the remotest areas and most pressing difficulties, has promised never to leave us or forsake us (see Heb. 13:5).

Third, charismatics emphasize *the power of the Holy Spirit*. They realize that the missionary enterprise must be advanced "not by might nor by power, but by My Spirit" (Zech. 4:6). For charismatics, the crucial requirement for effective missionaries is not education or cross-cultural expertise, as important as those factors are. The great prerequisite is to be filled with the Holy Spirit. Only after the Spirit comes upon us are we equipped to be witnesses to the ends of the earth. He fills us and progressively produces His fruit in us, traits that attract non-Christians. The love, joy, peace and patience produced by God's Spirit draw unbelievers. Through us, God "diffuses the fragrance of His knowledge in every place. For we are to God the fragrance of Christ among those who are being saved and among those who are perishing" (2 Cor. 2:14-15). All the gifts of the Holy Spirit enumerated in the Bible are at our disposal—including signs and wonders—to help propel the gospel worldwide.

Fourth, charismatic theology is underscored by a sense of *urgency*. With every tick of the clock, thousands fall into a Christless eternity. Charismatics cherish the eschatological hope of the full reign of Christ over planet Earth. They know that world evangelization is the prerequisite. Jesus said, "And this gospel of the kingdom will be preached in all the world as a witness to all nations, and then the end will come" (Matt. 24:14).

Windows of Opportunity

It is this pulsating urgency that can turn the charismatic movement into a major force in the earth. If we retain and even heighten our sense of immediacy, we can help deliver the entire body of Christ from the Scarlett O'Hara syndrome: "I'll think about that tomorrow!"

The dark side of the history of missions is the tragedy of missed opportunities. At the end of the Second World

War, General Douglas MacArthur pled with the American church to rush thousands of missionaries to a humbled, defeated Japan. Shintoism had failed them. Their "god," Hirohito, had just been "dedeified." It was a classic opportunity for Christianity to walk into a colossal spiritual vacuum. Instead we hesitated. In the minds of many American Christians, the Japanese were still "the enemy." And while we stalled, Japan groped toward a new religion—shameless, often vicious materialism. Is there a consequence, other than spiritual, when missions opportunities are lost? Every American pays every day for our spiritual failure in Japan.

I am tired of hearing about "closed doors" to the gospel. I agree with what one missions enthusiast said: "There are no closed doors to the gospel—provided that, once you get inside, you don't care if you ever come out!" Even if doors are closing, new windows of opportunity are opening all the time. The church must be poised to crawl rapidly through these seasonal open windows.

For a myriad of reasons, *glasnost* is a reality—at least for a while. There is a new openness for the gospel in the communist bloc. We cannot bank on long stretches of peace. In fact, Jesus said to expect the opposite as we approach the end of the age. He said, "You will hear of wars and rumors of wars" (Matt. 24:6). So in this short season of reprieve, we must move rapidly to spread the gospel. Is the church seizing this opportunity?

What about China—the "big apple" of missions with its billion plus people? The student unrest, in spite of its brutal suppression by hard-liners in the Chinese government, signals liberalization if not eventual democratization of that massive nation. Although recent, tragic events in China show a need for much more prayer for this troubled land, some missions researchers predict Western Christians will be able to reenter China on a missionary visa within a few years. But are we prepared—or even preparing? If we are truly serious about world evangelization, why aren't languages like Mandarin and Arabic major courses in our Bible colleges and seminaries?

Who in the church is prayerfully strategizing for the window of opportunity that will surely rise in Iran since the death of the Ayatollah Khomeini? Are we capitalizing on the fragile peace in Central America, South America and the Caribbean? Do we perceive the fresh gusts of the Spirit across Western Europe? Has it sunk in that the population of Nigeria (already Africa's most populous nation) will triple in fifty years? Do we remember that India will soon surpass China in population? Will we be there when Lebanon's long nightmare comes to an end? Are we taking advantage of areas where Christianity is already viewed favorably? Are we rushing in fresh troops to reap the full harvest where the Spirit is already mightily at work?

God help us to find answers. God help us even to ask the right questions!

A Renewal Strategy for Missions

As we prayerfully strategize to seize these and other opportunities, we should keep several facts in clear focus.

Fact Number 1: We must focus on the hidden peoples.
The most obvious goal of missions is to reach the unreached. I am excited about programs like Operation: Unreached, proposed by AIMS. Howard Foltz, president and founder of AIMS, is urging charismatic churches to ''adopt'' a specific unreached people and see it as their God-given responsibility to work until a viable church is planted in that group.

This definition of world evangelization—a church for every people—was first popularized by Ralph Winter, the initial genius and driving force behind the U.S. Center for World Mission. Winter comments,

> The God of the Bible confronts entire nationalities, challenges whole peoples, takes seriously every cultural sphere. And the God of the Bible doesn't talk about *most* of the people (individuals) of the world. God has not commanded us to go into *most* of the world. We do not read in the Bible that in the end times every tribe and tongue and people *with a few exceptions* will be represented. The Bible talks about *every people*— that is, every nation, tribe and tongue.[2]

Fact Number 2: We must concentrate on clusters of population. The largest city in the world, Mexico City, is within two or three hours by plane from most points in the United States. Why couldn't we bring a ''love assault'' of fifty thousand Spanish-speaking Christians, both Mexicans and Americans, into that city to canvass each dwelling with the gospel? Wayne Myers, Tim Ost and ministries like Every Home for Christ have done a spectacular job there. But I wonder what each could do with $10 million from caring American Christians.

Of course, both rural and urban areas need Christ. But often we have limited our witness to the "easier" rural or suburban areas. Are we afraid of the cities? Thank God, Floyd McClung has not been afraid to raise his family in the shadow of Amsterdam's infamous red-light district. Thank God, Mark Buntain exalted Jesus as the compassionate healer for the masses of Calcutta. Thank God, Mark Gregori defies the trend and pastors an Assembly of God church (and administers a Christian school) in the Bronx.

Recent statistics affirm that the total population of cities in Asia, Africa and Latin America already exceeds that of the cities in traditionally labeled "Western" and "communist" nations combined. U.N. projections anticipate meteoric growth during the next decade, so that by 2000 the population of those cities will surpass cities of the "Western" world by more than one billion.

How do we minister to these multitudes? Timothy M. Monsma, executive director of the Institute of Global Urban Studies, responds, "Western Christians must cast aside the stereotype that identifies mission work with rural living....We must proclaim the Gospel both by what we say and by what we do."[3]

Fact Number 3: We must train pastors and church workers in developing nations for their coming role as international church leaders. The implications of Howard Snyder's statement on the internationalization of the church must be seriously assessed. Since it is true that the church's dynamic center is shifting from North

Atlantic nations, we must do all we can to equip these anointed men and women from developing nations.

In my opinion, no Western preacher should conduct an evangelistic crusade in a developing nation unless he also does something significant for the church leaders there. Morris Cerullo has responded with his Schools of Evangelism. Dick Eastman has hosted Change the World Schools of Prayer for national church leaders before launching Every Home Crusades. Reinhard Bonnke has convened Eurofire conferences. Oral Roberts and Pat Robertson have founded schools that train some of the finest emerging leaders. And Billy Graham has sponsored great congresses on evangelism in Berlin, Lausanne and Amsterdam. He was also an initial force behind the ongoing Lausanne Committee on World Evangelization and its recent congress in Manila.

American Christians and churches can do much through sponsoring national projects and pastors' seminars and helping to produce training materials.

Fact Number 4: We must give priority to major un-reached groups. There must be those who will focus on the major blocs of unreached humanity while others focus on the subgroups within those blocs. I call this *macromissions* and *micromissions*. Both are vital. We thank God for the unprecedented reception of the gospel in China. When missionaries were forcibly evicted in the late 1940s, there were one million Chinese believers. Today there may be as many as eighty million. It is the greatest evangelistic miracle of the twentieth century. Nevertheless, that leaves over 920 million people in China without Jesus Christ. It is a major missions priority.

The masses of India, both Hindu and Muslim, will soon top one billion. This is another huge cluster of unreached humanity. India has some three thousand "subnations" and Christianity has as yet infiltrated fewer than one hundred of these.

Again there is the challenge of Islam. This religion too is edging toward the one billion mark. If we assume basic numerical parity between sexes, this means nearly one in every ten people in the world is a Muslim woman. This segment of the world's population is garrisoned against almost every conventional missionary approach. It would seem the only door of entry to these millions of women would be the compassionate friendship of Christian women.

Fact Number 5: World evangelization will require almost total mobilization of the church. In the famous statement from the Lausanne Covenant: "World evangelization requires the whole church to take the whole Gospel to the whole world."

Millions of Christians have not sensed their place in God's global plan. Virtually 99 percent of the church's human resources remain unemployed in evangelism. The great challenge of the church in the nineties is total mobilization. If and when every born-again believer senses the personal mandate to evangelize, we will soon evangelize the world.

Fact Number 6: The church will not be mobilized for missions without a large-scale revival. Thank God, this is beginning to happen. The "every nation army" of Christian soldiers is marching. Yes, we have been pruned. Admittedly, we have suffered some setbacks.

But let's not confuse losing battles with losing the war! The outcome of the cosmic warfare has already been determined. I pray and believe we are the generation that will rise and fulfill the Great Commission. But if we don't, some generation will. God has decreed it! The coming revival is not ultimately that we might feel better or even have a more decent society in which to live. The purpose of revival is to fire the church with divine energy for her divine assignment. Revival will tear us away from temporal pursuits to give ourselves for what really matters.

Fact Number 7: The church will not experience revival without large-scale intercession. Again, thank God, this is happening. World missions requires mobilization. But mobilization will not transpire without revival and revival will not occur without prayer. Prevailing prayer is always antecedent to revival. The great Bible commentator Matthew Henry said, "When God intends great blessing on His people, He sets them first a-praying." If this is true (and it is) we are on the threshold of great blessing. Intercession remains the unrivaled master key to fulfilling the Great Commission. Robert Speer, a great Presbyterian missions statesman, wrote,

> The evangelization of the world depends first upon a revival of prayer. Deeper than the need for workers; deeper, far, than the need for money; deep down at the bottom of our spiritual lives, is the need for the forgotten secret of prevailing, worldwide prayer. Missions have progressed slowly abroad because piety and

prayer have been shallow at home.[4]

Now piety and prayer are being restored.

The Holy Spirit, through a restored global church, will thrust in the sickle one last time to reap history's greatest harvest. We are only the firstfruits of the Spirit's outpouring. What will be the ultimate dimensions of the move of God's Spirit? God has promised, "I will pour out My Spirit on *all flesh*" (Joel 2:28).

TEN

To Whom Much Is Given

The charismatic renewal constitutes the most vital and fastest-growing movement in the church since the days of the Reformation.
—*Vinson Synan*

Some years ago Naomi and I walked into the small bedroom of a home in Toronto. There, bedfast and in his nineties, lay the greatest missionary statesman of the twentieth century, Oswald J. Smith. When he saw us, his countenance brightened and he greeted us warmly. Then, looking at me with his piercing eyes, he inquired, ''Young man, what are you doing for missions?'' The question nips at my conscience every day.

Smith's life and ministry had touched me for years

before I met him. His gospel songs, including "The Song of the Soul Set Free" and "Then Jesus Came," had always lifted me. But it was his books that stirred me most. When I was in high school, T.L. Osborn gave me a copy of Smith's *The Passion for Souls*. In its gripping pages I was confronted with the challenge, "Why should anyone hear the gospel twice until everyone has heard it once?" To this day I cannot give a credible answer.

After several minutes we prepared to leave. "Dr. Smith," I almost whispered, "I believe there is spiritual significance in the laying on of hands. Sir, would you lay hands on me and pray that your missions passion will be mine as well?"

As he placed his hand on my head and prayed, that little room became a cathedral for me. The presence of God flooded my heart. I left with a fresh sense that I was a debtor to my generation.

Who's Accountable?

Once after I preached on our missions responsibility, an obviously irritated woman approached me. "What does that have to do with me?" she snapped. "What do needy children in Africa have to do with my needs? Who made me accountable?"

She had cornered herself with her own questions. Who indeed has made us accountable? Our Lord and God. I do not wish to be unkind. Nevertheless, I admit that priority number one for too many of us is not the glory of God but the blessing of ourselves. Some have been infested with a "Cain mentality." The Cain mentality quips, "Am I my brother's keeper?" The Jesus mentality responds, "My nourishment is to do the will of the Father and finish His work." We must resonate Paul's heartbeat: "I am a debtor both to Greeks and to barbarians, both to wise and to unwise. So, as much as is in me, I am ready to preach the gospel..." (Rom. 1:14-15).

Let us suppose we as charismatics are the most blessed wing of Christianity. (We may not be, but let's just suppose.) Suppose we do excel in spiritual gifts. What if our spiritual sensitivity is indeed advanced beyond other brethren? Let's assume that we do, in fact, exercise more faith than others. Suppose the statistics are right that we are indeed the most vital and fastest-growing bloc of Christians. *Does it not then follow that we are most accountable for the evangelization of the world?* Jesus said, "For everyone to whom much is given, from him much will be required; and to whom much has been committed, of him they will ask the more" (Luke 12:48).

Without a doubt, we are a blessed people. We have been given much. And much will be required of us. Our emphasis on faith must now be rechanneled to believe God for entire nations to come under the sway of the gospel. I can't repeat this verse too often: "Ask of Me, and I will give You the nations for Your inheritance, and the ends of the earth for Your possession" (Ps. 2:8). Ted Engstrom, president emeritus of World Vision, noted correctly, "A congregation which is not deeply and earnestly involved in the world-wide proclamation of the Gospel does not understand the nature of salvation."[1]

A noted missions leader once asked a pastor, "What do your people most need to be mobilized for world evangelism?" He pondered a moment and answered, "A staggering view of God." As those whose Christian experience thrives on praise and worship of the awe-inspiring God, may our throne room be moved to the harvest fields.

The Posture of a Servant

In 1988 I was honored to meet with President Daniel Moi of Kenya in the State House in Nairobi. As I sat in the drawing room of that beautiful building, I mused how profoundly times had changed. That majestic structure had been built early in this century as a monument to British rule in East Africa. The British have long since been evicted, and the home they built to shield themselves from the people now belongs to the people of Kenya. The tables have been turned dramatically.

This reality must ring with clarity in the minds and hearts of all Christians from Western nations who would minister in other lands. Nationals have a keen ability to sniff out any vestiges of imperialism, provincialism or paternalism remaining in us. It would be both unscriptural and unworkable for any Western missionary to assume arrogance in a nation where he or she lives and works as a guest. Missionaries are servants, not lords. There is only one Lord. As His emissaries, missionaries must posture themselves as servants of Jesus Christ, the national church and its indigenous leadership.

When I minister overseas, I cannot hide the fact that I am an American. But that is not my first point of identity. My identity, first and foremost, is as a Christian. My culture, compared to any other culture, is superior only insofar as the gospel has touched and transformed it. Missionaries are not superior people. All people are of equal worth to God. Nor do missionaries necessarily come from a superior culture. But they *do* proclaim a superior message and a superior way of life through Jesus Christ.

Some years ago I was talking to a businessman seated next to me on a plane. In the course of our conversation, he asked me, "What do you do?" I responded, "I'm an ambassador."

Surprised, he inquired further, "What country do you represent? The United States?"

I replied, "No, I represent a kingdom far more powerful than the United States. I represent the kingdom of God!"

So do you, whether you're in your hometown or half a world away. "We are ambassadors for Christ, as though God were pleading through us: we implore you on Christ's behalf, be reconciled to God" (2 Cor. 5:20).

If we truly belong to Christ, wherever we go we represent Him. We may do so poorly, but we represent Him nonetheless. Years ago a book called *The Ugly American* confronted many Americans with their often insensitive behavior toward the rest of the world. God protect us from being "ugly Christians" because of unbiblical, un-Christian words and deeds in cross-cultural situations.

Jesus said,

> You know that those who are considered rulers over the Gentiles lord it over them, and their

great ones exercise authority over them.

Yet it shall not be so among you; but whoever desires to become great among you shall be your servant.

And whoever of you desires to be first shall be slave of all.

For even the Son of Man did not come to be served, but to serve, and to give His life as a ransom for many (Mark 10:42-45).

Motives for Missions

In all our activity, the bottom line is that we do what we are stirred to do. Are there some hidden drives that can propel us into greater missions involvement? Indeed, there are.

First, as I've already mentioned, we should be involved in missions out of a *sense of debt*. Paul felt acutely indebted to his generation. He exposes one of the great driving forces of his life when he says, "I am a debtor..." (Rom. 1:14). Those enlightened by the gospel have a profound responsibility to those still in darkness. When we understand our debt, we too will say, "I am ready to preach the gospel....I am not ashamed of the gospel of Christ" (Rom. 1:15-16).

Second, we should be involved in missions out of a *sense of devotion*. "For Christ's love compels us" (2 Cor. 5:14, NIV). Christ's love for us and our love for Him always thrust us into the harvest. There is no such thing as Christian discipleship that is nonevangelistic. According to Jesus Himself, the result of following Him is that we become fishers of men and women (see Matt. 4:19).

158

Third, we should feel a *sense of duty*. The late R.G. Lee, the great Southern Baptist pulpiteer, said, "The biggest word in the English language is *duty*." Yet it is a word and a concept almost lost to our generation. There are some things we simply must do. Winston Churchill, at the height of the Second World War, challenged his countrymen, "We must do more than our best. We must do what is required." It is simply required that we now plant the lordship of Jesus in all the earth. Paul said, "Necessity is laid upon me; yes, woe is me if I do not preach the gospel!" (1 Cor. 9:16).

Fourth, being actively involved in missions produces in us a *sense of direction*. World evangelization becomes an integrating theme around which all other concerns orbit. When interrogated by King Agrippa, Paul was able to reply,

> I was not disobedient to the heavenly vision, but declared first to those in Damascus and in Jerusalem, and throughout all the region of Judea, and then to the Gentiles, that they should repent, turn to God, and do works befitting repentance (Acts 26:19-20).

Missions involvement allows us to live for what really matters—the heavenly vision of Christ's lordship saturating the earth.

Finally, missions involvement gives us a *sense of destiny*. We are a chosen generation. God has allowed our lives to intersect with the most exciting time in all history. We have the privilege of helping set the time-table of heaven's eschatology. In times like these, God's

Word calls us to a fresh commitment to both holiness and evangelism. "Therefore, since all these things will be dissolved, what manner of persons ought you to be in holy conduct and godliness, looking for and hastening the coming of the day of God" (2 Pet. 3:11-12). Amazingly, Scripture tells us that we can help hasten that great day when Christ's rule will be complete.

Catching a World Vision

All right, you may be saying, I'm convinced I should be more deeply involved. But how? What concrete steps do I take?

I'm glad you asked! There are several steps you can take, starting as soon as you put this book down.

First, *give sacrificially*. A greater heart for missions starts in the purse and pocketbook. Why? Because Jesus said that our hearts always follow our treasure.

> Do not lay up for yourselves treasures on earth, where moth and rust destroy and where thieves break in and steal; but lay up for yourselves treasures in heaven, where neither moth nor rust destroys and where thieves do not break in and steal.
>
> For where your treasure is, there your heart will be also (Matt. 6:19-21).

Give sacrificially to your church's missions program, individual missionaries, credible mission agencies and ministries to the poor. Treasures in heaven are the soundest investment on earth!

Second, *pray globally*. Years ago Ruth Graham was

asked if she used a prayer book in her devotions. "Yes," she replied, "the morning newspaper." Every major event affects the gospel either favorably or adversely. So pray over current events. Pray too for countries in a systematic way. I use Dick Eastman's World Prayer Map and Patrick Johnstone's *Operation World* as aids to global intercession.[2] Don't forget to pray by name for missionaries and national workers, lifting their needs to God. Then pray specifically for unreached peoples. The *Global Prayer Digest* provided by Frontier Fellowship is excellent for this purpose.[3] Youth With a Mission provides a terrific daily prayer journal for the nations and unreached people.[4] Nothing connects you with the purposes of God more than catching the Holy Spirit's intercession as He sweeps over the earth to accomplish God's agenda.

Third, *read widely*. There has been an explosion of excellent missions literature in the last few years. The bibliography at the back of this book offers some suggestions. But even that selective list may seem overwhelming. So allow me to offer some personal suggestions. To see what God is doing in the world today, read *On the Crest of the Wave* by Peter Wagner. *Perspectives on the World Christian Movement*, edited by Ralph Winter and Steven Hawthorne, is an invaluable resource covering the gamut of missions. An excellent history of missions focusing on the lives of those God has used is Ruth Tucker's *From Jerusalem to Irian Jaya*. Bruce Olson has written an exciting, contemporary story, *Bruchko*, of his adventures evangelizing the Motilone tribe. For missionary stories, *Shadow of the Almighty* by Elisabeth Elliot is the classic story of her martyred first husband, Jim Elliot. One of my favorite missions books is *Eternity in Their Hearts* by Don Richardson.

Fourth, *think globally and eternally.* Most people are geared to think and live in a temporal, local framework. It will take a conscientious refocusing to move in the other direction. There is an immediate payoff for a global, eternal orientation. Many things that wouldn't "fit" in life begin to fit. A lot of questions are answered and a lot of loose ends are tied up neatly.

Fifth, *go personally.* For many people, going out of town is not an option, much less going overseas. But we live in an increasingly mobile world. Technology has turned us into a global village. I'm told that at any given time there are some eight million Americans in other countries. If there is a potential of travel for you, there are several options.

To serve the Lord in another land or in an area here that needs your love, you don't have to be called to be a missionary. Perhaps you could invest your vacation in missions. Consider a missions trip sponsored by your church. Perhaps you work for a multinational company. You could pray about an overseas transfer. You may have a skill that is needed in developing nations. Services such as Intercristo and Tentmakers International can help you match your skills with the world's needs.

There are vast opportunities for short-term service, especially for youth. This is where much of the action is in missions expansion. Most missions organizations provide short-term opportunities ranging from a month to two years. Your church may be involved in summer outreaches overseas. Agencies such as Teen Missions, Youth With a Mission and AIMS can also provide information on missions expeditions.

Sixth, *love cross-culturally*. If you can't go overseas, take heart. The world is also coming to you! World Ambassadors, an outreach of Bob Weiner's Maranatha Ministries, and International Students provide excellent avenues for caring involvement.

Thousands of tomorrow's leaders of nations are studying in our country right now. Most international students desperately want American friends. You can be their link with the love of Christ. Thousands of students leave America and Britain disappointed. They had wanted to discover the truths of Christianity and the people of the nation. Too often, they find neither.

Finally, *work differently*. However you acquire your necessary finances, your true vocation as a Christian is to love God and make Him loved, to know God and make Him known. "And whatever you do, do it heartily, as to the Lord and not to men" (Col. 3:23). Wherever you are, you represent the Lord Jesus Christ and are part of the fabric of His master design. Every day Christians are spread out over the nations as the salt of the earth and the light of the world. "Let your light so shine before men, that they may see your good works and glorify your Father in heaven" (Matt. 5:16).

Cut the Coal!

You—yes, you—are vital to the fulfilling of God's purposes in the earth. No one can touch your sphere of influence as you can. There is a "world" only you can reach. And there is a role in the worldwide Christian advance that only you can play.

During the Second World War, Winston Churchill, then prime minister of Great Britain, set out to "win with words" over Hitler by raising the morale of the nation. Not only did he visit troops and factories, but he went to the out-of-the-way coal-mining towns. On one visit to the hard-working coal miners, the prime minister urged them to see their significance in the total effort for victory. He told them:

> "We will be victorious! We will preserve our freedom. And years from now when our freedom is secure and peace reigns, your children and children's children will come and they will say to you, 'What did you do to win our freedom in that great war?' And one will say, 'I marched with the Eighth Army!' Someone else will proudly say, 'I manned a submarine.' And another will say, 'I guided the ships that moved the troops and the supplies.' And still another will say, 'I doctored the wounds!'
>
> Then the great statesman paused. The dirty-faced miners sat in silence and awe, waiting for him to proceed.
>
> "They will come to you," he shouted, "and you will say, with equal right and equal pride, 'I cut the coal! I cut the coal that fueled the ships that moved the supplies! That's what I did. I cut the coal!' "[5]

Ever since Jesus chose His undeserving disciples, the

spread of Christianity has often been in the hands of those who would most likely be passed up by leadership scouts. The prayers of the elderly on fixed incomes, the compassion of Christian homemakers, the unbridled evangelistic passion of youth—these are the "coal cutters" in the real war.

You may never stand before masses and preach the gospel. You may not trudge through hostile territory to carry the gospel to remote villages. You may never leave your native soil. But you can cut the coal! Your Christlike integrity, your bold intercession and your sacrificial giving will fuel the advance of Christ's kingdom worldwide.

"Today, If You Will Hear His Voice..."

The Holy Spirit is speaking to hearts as never before about taking part in the global harvest. But not only must individuals heed this fresh word of the Lord. Whole churches, networks of churches and denominations must hear this present word. God is bellowing *global harvest* for those who have ears to hear.

For the last decade I have been privileged to work side-by-side with my friend and pastor, Larry Lea. He echoes the same urgent message. In his book *The Hearing Ear*, Lea states,

> Tides and currents are shifting. Dangerous shoals and treacherous reefs are lying in wait. New winds are blowing. If the church is to move forward in the flow of God, she must catch the fresh wind of the Spirit. The people of God must

set their courses by the unwavering, sure revelation of the Holy Spirit. We must hear and obey what the Spirit is saying to the churches.[6]

"Therefore, as the Holy Spirit says: 'Today, if you will hear His voice, do not harden your hearts' " (Heb. 3:7). Today, if we hear what the Spirit is saying to the churches, *our commitment to Christ will be stronger than ever*. We will deal ruthlessly with our carnality and crown Jesus as Lord of all. We will never again be brought to shame because of lethargy, sectarianism and flirtations with the spirit of the age. We will offer ourselves unreservedly to Christ, to spend and be spent that His rule may be established over the entire earth. We will not care whether we live in affluence or need. We will not be derailed by either criticism or accolades. Knowing that our times are in His hands, we will not care whether we live or die—if only the gospel is advanced. "For if we live, we live to the Lord; and if we die, we die to the Lord. Therefore, whether we live or die, we are the Lord's" (Rom. 14:8).

If we hear the "now word" of the Holy Spirit, *our giving to missions will be greater than ever*. We will not be part of the "pig in a python," the term some demographers have given to the vast swell of baby-boomers as they move through the snake of time. While we will believe God for fiscal strength greater than ever, we will renounce materialism and its deadening effects. At a pace unprecedented in Christian history, we will translate our money into new churches, food for the hungry, schools, literature and medical clinics around the world.

If we hear His voice, *our going will be in larger numbers than ever.* The Christian missionary force will swell, not only with new recruits from Western nations but with thousands of missionaries from developing nations. Wherever we are, at home or away, we will feel acutely the privilege of being His ambassadors. The worldwide body of Christ will awaken each new day with an appreciation of its missionary assignment. With fresh, holy longing, Christians will clamor for selection when the Lord asks, "Whom shall I send, and who will go for Us?" Vast numbers will volunteer: "Here am I. Send me" (Is. 6:8).

And when we respond to the Spirit's urging, *our praying will be more forceful than ever.* We will command demon hierarchies to release their ancient grip over peoples and nations. We will say to the North, "Give them up!" And to the South, "Do not keep them back! Bring God's sons from afar, and His daughters from the ends of the earth—everyone who is called by His name" (see Is. 43:6-7). We will dispatch angels to fight in the heavenlies and minister to the heirs of salvation. By our prayers we will help orchestrate the reaping of the final harvest. We will fight and win through our prayers. We will aggressively love the last, the least, the lost. But we will aggressively hate every work of darkness.

A century ago a battered batallion of weary soldiers was being pushed back toward imminent defeat. With men falling on every side, the general ordered the bugler to sound the retreat. But there was no bugler; he had just been killed. Anxiously the general inquired if anyone could blow the bugle. One young recruit responded yes.

"Well, sound the retreat," the general ordered.

"Sir," the new bugler responded, "I don't know how to blow the retreat. I only know how to blow the charge."

"Then blow the charge!" And with the blowing of the charge, the troops were energized, the tide was turned, and victory rose out of sure defeat.

The Holy Spirit is enlivening the church to produce a force in the earth that does not know how to blow the retreat. While some may think circumstances call for retreat, we only know how to blow the charge. The battle is hot. The global situation is less than favorable. But the Spirit of God is commanding us to advance. Victory is inevitable.

"For the earth shall be full of the knowledge of the Lord as the waters cover the sea" (Is. 11:9).

Notes

Chapter 1

1. D.B. Barrett, "Statistics, Global." *Dictionary of the Pentecostal and Charismatic Movements*. Stanley M. Burgess and Gary B. McGee, editors. (Grand Rapids: Zondervan, 1988), pp. 810-830.

Chapter 3

1. D. Martyn Lloyd-Jones, *Joy Unspeakable* (Eastbourne, England: Kingsway, 1984), p. 75.

2. C. Peter Wagner, "Special Kinds of Church Growth" (Class notes, Fuller Theological Seminary, 1984), p. 14.

3. John Wimber with Kevin Springer, *Power Evangelism* (San Francisco: Harper & Row, 1986), p. 16.

4. T.L. Osborn, *The Harvest Call* (Tulsa: The Voice of Faith, 1953), p. 143.

5. C. Peter Wagner, *The Third Wave of the Holy Spirit* (Ann Arbor: Vine Books, 1988), p. 87.

6. Charles E. Kraft, *Christianity with Power* (Ann Arbor: Vine Books, 1989), p. 110.

7. Quoted by Arthur Johnstone, *The Battle for World Evangelism* (Wheaton, Ill.: Tyndale House, 1978), p. 30.

8. T.L. Osborn, *The Purpose of Pentecost* (Tulsa: Osborn Foundation, 1963), p. 105.

9. Wimber and Springer, p. 31.

Chapter 4

1. Leighton Ford, *The Christian Persuader* (New York: Harper & Row, 1966), p. 29.

2. Quoted by Arthur Johnstone, *The Battle for World Evangelism* (Wheaton, Ill.: Tyndale House Publishers, 1978), p. 168.

3. Jon Braun, *Whatever Happened to Hell?* (Nashville: Thomas Nelson Inc., Publishers, 1979), pp. 105-106.

4. Dick Hillis, *What If They Haven't Heard?* (Chicago: Moody Press, 1986), pp. 20-21.

Chapter 5

1. Norman Grubb, *Rees Howells, Intercessor* (Fort Washington, Pa.: Christian Literature Crusade, 1979).

2. Paul Billheimer, *The Technique of Spiritual Warfare* (Santa Ana, Calif.: TBN Press, 1982), p. 58.

3. Dick Eastman, *Love on Its Knees* (Old Tappan, N.J.: Chosen Books, 1989), p. 19.

4. Quoted in the tract *Prayer Is the Lifeline of Missions* (The Great Commission Prayer League).

5. S.D. Gordon, *Quiet Talks on Prayer* (Pyramid Publications, 1967), p. 27.

6. J. Edwin Orr, lecture to pastors at a European leadership conference, Zurich, Switzerland, May 1986.

7. Paul Y. Cho, *Prayer: Key to Revival* (Waco, Tex.: Word Books, 1984), p. 106.

8. Ole Hallesby, *Prayer* (Minneapolis: Augsburg Publishing House, 1959), p. 131.

9. E.M. Bounds, *Power Through Prayer* (Chicago: Moody Press, 1979), p. 94.

Chapter 6

1. Quoted in Arthur Johnstone, *The Battle for World Evangelism* (Wheaton, Ill.: Tyndale House Publishers, 1978), pp. 165-166.

2. C. Peter Wagner, *On the Crest of the Wave* (Glendale, Calif.: Regal Books, 1983), p. 9.

3. Wagner, p. 171.

4. David B. Barrett, ed., *World Christian Encyclopedia*: A Comparative Study of Churches and Religions in the Modern World

A.D. 1900-2000 (Nairobi, Kenya: Oxford University Press, 1982), p. 3.

5. Howard R. Snyder with Daniel V. Runyon, *Foresight*: Ten Major Trends That Will Dramatically Affect the Future of Christians and the Church (Nashville: Thomas Nelson Publishers, 1986), p. 25.

6. Jack Hayford, "The Lausanne Covenant and I," *World Evangelization*, January 1989, p. 13.

7. John R. Mott, Lectures to Rochester, New York, YMCA staff, March 1943.

8. Paul Borthwick, *Youth and Missions* (Wheaton, Ill.: SP Publications Inc., 1988), p. 29.

9. Tony Campolo, "The Passionless Generation," *Youthworker Journal*, Summer 1985, p. 20.

Chapter 7

1. David J. Hesselgrave, "The Millennium and Missions," *Evangelical Missions Quarterly*, Volume 24, Number 1 (January 1988), p. 76.

2. Richard F. Lovelace, *Dynamics of Spiritual Life* (Downers Grove, Ill.: InterVarsity Press, 1979), pp. 424-425.

Chapter 8

1. Jerry Cook, *Love, Acceptance & Forgiveness* (Glendale, Calif.: Regal Books, 1979), p. 125.

2. Quoted by L. Grant McClung Jr., "Theology and Strategy of Pentecostal Missions," *International Bulletin of Missionary Research*, January 1988, p. 4.

Chapter 9

1. David Watson, *I Believe in Evangelism* (Grand Rapids: William B. Eerdmans, 1977).

2. Ralph D. Winter, "Countdown 2000!" *World Evangelization*, November-December 1988, p. 7.

3. Timothy M. Monsma, "Urbanization Now and at the Turn of the Millennium," *World Evangelization*, March-April 1989, pp. 28-29.

4. Quoted by Dick Eastman, *Love on Its Knees* (Old Tappan,

N.J.: Chosen Books, 1989), pp. 175-176.

Chapter 10

1. Ted W. Engstrom, *What in the World Is God Doing?* (Waco, Tex.: Word Inc., 1978), p. 197.

2. The World Prayer Map may be obtained by writing Every Home for Christ, P.O. Box 7139, Canoga Park, CA 91324-7139. *Operation World* by Patrick Johnstone is published by STL Books, P.O. Box 28, Waynesboro, GA 30830.

3. *Global Prayer Digest*, published in cooperation with the Frontier Fellowship, may be obtained from the Association of International Mission Services (AIMS), P.O. Box 64534, Virginia Beach, VA 23464.

4. Contact Youth With a Mission, P.O. Box 4600, Tyler, TX 75712.

5. Quoted by Ted W. Engstrom and Robert C. Larson, *Seizing the Torch* (Glendale, Calif.: Regal Books, 1988), p. 72.

6. Larry Lea, *The Hearing Ear* (Altamonte Springs, Fla.: Creation House, 1988), p. 12.

A Select Missions Bibliography

General Missions

Borthwick, Paul. *A Mind for Missions*. Colorado Springs: NavPress, 1987.

-------. *Youth and Missions*. Wheaton: Victor, 1988.

Bryant, David. *In the Gap: What It Means to Be a World Christian*. Glendale, Calif.: Regal, 1979.

DuBose, Francis M., editor. *Classics of Christian Missions*. Nashville: Broadman, 1979.

Eastman, Dick. *Love on Its Knees*. Old Tappan, N.J.: Chosen, 1989.

Engstrom, Ted W., and Larson, Robert C. *Seizing the Torch*. Glendale, Calif.: Regal, 1988.

Hodges, Melvin L. *The Indigenous Church*. Springfield, Mo.: Gospel Publishing House, 1976.

Kane, J. Herbert. *A Concise History of the Christian World Mission*. Grand Rapids: Baker, 1978.

-------. *Wanted: World Christians*. Grand Rapids: Baker, 1986.

Kyle, John E., compiler. *The Unfinished Task*. Glendale, Calif.: Regal, 1984.

Neill, Stephen. *A History of Christian Missions*. New York: Penguin, 1964.

Richardson, Don. *Eternity in Their Hearts*. Glendale, Calif.: Regal, 1984.

Tucker, Ruth A. *From Jerusalem to Irian Jaya*. Grand Rapids: Zondervan, 1986.

Wagner, C. Peter. *On the Crest of the Wave: Becoming a World Christian*. Glendale, Calif.: Regal, 1983.

Wilson, J. Christy, Jr. *Today's Tentmakers*. Wheaton: Tyndale House, 1979.

Winter, Ralph D., and Hawthorne, Steven C., editors. *Perspectives on the World Christian Movement*. Pasadena: William Carey, 1981.

Yohannan, K.P. *The Coming Revolution in World Missions*. Altamonte Springs, Fla.: Creation House, 1986.

Charismatics and Missions

Boer, Harry R. *Pentecost and Missions*. Grand Rapids: William B. Eerdmans, 1961.

Burgess, Stanley M., and McGee, Gary B., editors. *Dictionary of Pentecostal and Charismatic Movements*. Grand Rapids: Zondervan, 1988.

Kraft, Charles H. *Christianity with Power*. Ann Arbor: Vine Books, 1989.

McClung, L. Grant, Jr., editor. *Azusa Street and Beyond*. South Plainfield, N.J.: Bridge, 1986.

Osborn, T.L. *Healing the Sick*. Tulsa: Harrison House, 1981.

Osborn, T.L. *The Purpose of Pentecost*. Tulsa: Osborn Foundation, 1963.

Pomerville, Paul A. *The Third Force in Missions*. Peabody, Mass.: Hendrickson, 1985.

Synan, Vinson. *The Twentieth-Century Pentecostal Explosion*. Altamonte Springs, Fla.: Creation House, 1987.

Wagner, C. Peter. *Church Growth and the Whole Gospel*. San Francisco: Harper & Row, 1981.

-------. *Spiritual Power and Church Growth* Altamonte Springs, Fla.: Creation House, 1986. Published previously as *What Are We Missing?* and *Look Out! The Pentecostals Are Coming!*

-------. *The Third Wave of the Holy Spirit*. Ann Arbor: Vine Books, 1988.

Missionary Stories

Baldwin, Lindley. *Samuel Morris*. Minneapolis: Bethany House, 1987.

Burke, Todd and DeAnn. *Anointed for Burial*. South Plainfield, N.J.: Bridge, 1977.

Cunningham, Loren. *Is That Really You, God?* Old Tappan, N.J.: Chosen, 1984.

Elliot, Elisabeth. *A Chance to Die: The Life and Legacy of Amy Carmichael*. Old Tappan, N.J.: Fleming H. Revell, 1987.

-------. *Shadow of the Almighty: The Life and Testament of Jim Elliot*. New York: Harper and Brothers, 1958.

Estes, Steve. *Called to Die: The Story of American Linguist Chet Bitterman*. Grand Rapids: Zondervan, 1986.

Garlock, H.B. *Before We Kill and Eat You*. Dallas: Christ for the Nations, 1974.

Graham, Franklin, with Lockerbie, Jeanette. *Bob Pierce: This One Thing I Do*. Waco, Tex.: Word, 1983.

Hefley, James and Marti. *Uncle Cam: The Story of William Cameron Townsend*. Milford, Mich.: Mott Media, 1981.

Kinnear, Angus I. *Against the Tide: The Story of Watchman Nee*. Fort Washington, Penn.: Christian Literature Crusade, 1973.

Lake, John G. *Adventures in God*. Tulsa: Harrison House, 1981.

Neely, Lois. *Fire in His Bones: The Biography of Oswald J. Smith*. Wheaton: Tyndale House, 1982.

Olson, Bruce E. *Bruchko*. Altamonte Springs, Fla.: Creation House, 1978.

Osborn, T.L. and Daisy. *The Gospel According to T.L. and Daisy*. Tulsa: Osborn Foundation, 1985.

Shibley, David and Naomi. *The Smoke of a Thousand Villages—and Other Stories of Real Life Heroes of the Faith*. Nashville: Thomas Nelson, 1989.

Taylor, L.J. Hudson. *Hudson Taylor*. Minneapolis: Bethany, 1987.

Weiner, Bob. *Take Dominion*. Old Tappan, N.J.: Chosen, 1988.

Mission Courses for the Church

Mission Dynamics. Available from the Association of International Mission Services (AIMS), P.O. Box 64534, Virginia Beach, VA 23464.

Perspectives on the World Christian Movement. Available from the U.S. Center for World Mission, 1605 Elizabeth Street, Pasadena, CA 91104.